Mining the Mine!

A DIY Plan to Finding the Hidden Treasures in Your Home

By Alexa Keating

Revised 2020

Prologue

Do you believe that the longest journey begins with the first step? Maybe it begins before that. I believe that when something matters to us a lot, we harbor a dream. Holding onto that dream can be difficult but will only become impossible when we refuse to dare to dream.

Your dream, when held close to your heart, fans a tiny flame, a pilot light that ignites hope. What does this have to do with mining? Your home is your sanctuary, your safe space. Regardless of budgetary or other limitations it needs to feel comforting. 'Mining the Mine' guides the reader through discovering what creates those emotions within and how to make it happen.

Hope springs to life when we begin to believe that there might be a way to accomplish the dream. Once we believe in the dream, we begin to realize that dream. And so it is.

Introduction

'Mining the Mine goes beyond home decorating as it delves into the nuts and bolts of how to make all those 'dreamed of' projects become a new reality!

Together we take a closer look at what you have and what you would like to have to make your space feel relaxing and secure. Next we will examine how to use what you have, to do what you can, where you are. The final result is creating an entirely new look on a minimal budget. The information shared ensures a wonderful, lighthearted approach to a final finish on budget.

Every home is a personal expression of the people who live there. 'Mining the Mine' guides you ever so subtly, as you delve into your family's lifestyle, helping you to decide exactly what you need from the space and what you really want to create in your home. Once you have determined your goal, this book will lead you effortlessly (almost!) to your objective.

'Mining the Mine' shares hundreds of ideas to help you improve your home; this is a must read! It is the new 'survival bible' for recreating personal spaces and repurposing furniture in your home.

Table of Contents

Dedication

This book was inspired by and written for all the people who wish they could create their dream home, have limited funds to commit to your ideas, and don't quite know where to start or how to make it happen!

This is not simply an instructional manual. 'Mining the Mine' it is more like a best friend working side by side with you to bring your dreams to realization. There's a difference.

Together we will define your personal style and recreate your new dream from what you already have... by mining your mine!

Chapter 1
It's About Time!

Have you ever taken a long look around your home and wondered how it all came to this? If so, now is the time to rein in the confusion and begin again... it's about time!

We begin space planning and design with such vast hopes and dreams. We go shopping in various places or collect hand me downs from a relative only to end up with a result that screams 'not me!'

Or worse, you look around at a room full of odds and ends and what, in your eyes, appears to be 'early junk' furniture and decide you hate it all. A second look at your expendable income that can be used to transform the room into something that feels desirable can leave you feeling rather hopeless.

This is where the fun begins. This book is designed to help you take a thoughtful approach to each room in your home. Together we will decide exactly what the purpose of the room is going to serve, what you need the space to accomplish in your home and what 'look and feel' of the energy in the room suits you and your lifestyle best. Next we will take a new look at what you have to work with to create the ideal space. Then, we go to work!

Some thoughts to remember before we begin; I discovered a few things that seem to be the 'norm' in every home, maybe yours aa well.

Some pieces of furniture and accessories are sacred. They were given to you by someone special and you plan to never let them go, no matter what. You may be open to re-purposing them into something magnificent when we are finished.

There are a few pieces of furniture and accessories that you likely picked up at yard sales, thrift stores or bought from a friend as you began your decorating plan. We can do great things with these!

You probably also have some new pieces of furniture and accessories that you fell in love with or got a great deal on but they just don't look the way you hoped they would. We will work together to determine where these pieces can shine in your plan.

You've probably had a lot of this 'stuff' before you moved into your current space. 'Mining the Mine' will help you make a decision about what can be used, what can be re-purposed and what you may want to sell to acquire the funds for new pieces you consider a new 'must have.'

If any of these circumstances apply to you and your home, consider yourself 'normal.' A cautionary note; there is an issue that is perhaps not so much the 'norm' but makes life very uncomfortable in our homes; a husband with one very distinct style that makes him feel comfortable and a wife with a completely different style. Typically, each of these partners believes their style is best.

This kind of situation can create so much conflict in your home that no style ever develops. Many times it actually escalates to a place where one of the partners has begun to question their own sense of style, or has given up on gaining control of their surroundings to avoid arguments or painful interaction. This can feel defeating.

If this is your situation I urge you to select a room that both of you have agreed is under your control; a space that is either not shared (like a bedroom) or a space where you spend the primary amount of time and therefore can be expected to gain some control over the character of the room.

Later we will address the other members in your household and how to include them in the plans. Today, we rediscover YOU!

Choose A Room; Any Room!

If you are unsure where to start, begin where you are the most uncomfortable in your home; a space that makes you feel unwelcome, is uninviting and even perhaps just plain ugly. That's the one!

You may even find yourself in a situation where you have no choice; things have to change! This typically comes about when you have a new addition to your household. Maybe something has changed like children in college who need a different kind of space, a new job that requires an office to work from or elderly parents as your children leaving the nest.

Suddenly you need something different to make your home function and feel user friendly.

There are all kinds of reasons but if this is your situation then you already know where to start.

Your goal will be far easier to reach if you are able to clear the room of all of the furniture and accessories. If that is not possible, move everything to the center of the room and visually 'clear the room.' (It's the effect of clearing the decks!)

Grab a tablet to make notes and your favorite drink and find a comfortable place to sit down. You may like sitting on the floor in a sunbeam!

This is the beginning of a journey that will take you step-by-step from A to Z and will result in a finished room that is totally YOU!

Take a deep breath and look around you. Notice the natural lighting that is available in the room, which direction the windows are facing, where the doorways are and any 'unusual' features in your room. Make a note of these issues.

Unusual in this instance means any wall that is broken by closets, built-ins or anything else that prevents the wall from being a straight wall. This is important!

Some examples of challenging architectural designs are:

Irregular shapes
Fireplace oddly jutting out.
Angular and unusable spaces
Odd, narrow corners and excessive doors
Triangle shapes from bedroom entry
Angled ceilings, tiny spaces
Bay windows in an inconvenient location
Long, narrow open spaces (typically found in Cape Cod Style home or a home where the attic was finished out).

Next decide whether you want those nooks and crannies to be hidden or emphasized. If they are attractive or give the room character, you may want to show them off. If they reflect a completely different style than the one you choose for the room, you may want to intentionally ignore them. First decide how they make you feel, then you are ready to decide whether to emphasize or diminish them in your new look.

If you find that your personal style is contemporary or minimalist you will most likely feel more comfortable allowing these unusual spaces to blend into the décor rather than showcasing them. Paint color, floor treatments, window treatments and furniture placement all work together to create the style you choose.

Even though it may be difficult, at this point you may be better off to ignore the existing furniture. Focusing on the furniture may cause you to limit your personal style by what you see in the room or what you believe you have to work with. It is an easy trap to fall into; don't do it!

This is a new awakening. Together we begin again and this time, we will create the look and feeling of a space you can love.

Chapter 2
Who Done It?

I have had the opportunity to meet many people on my life path. Every single person has had an encounter with a culprit named 'not me.'

You meet this scoundrel at work when something is missing and no one moved it, at home when you suddenly find mud caked on the white carpet and in a multitude of other places along the way. Wherever something has happened and no one want to assume responsibility for the actions, you'll find he's been there; the one and only 'not me.' You may have to tolerate that out in the world, but who let him into your home?

If things feel unbalanced or out of control in our lives, it is frequently reflected in our homes. Likewise, if we want to correct that in our lives, the home is the best place to begin. Why? Because it is our refuge; your home is the place where you lock out the intruders in your life and let your hair down. It is a sacred sanctity where we go for inner healing and peace of mind. These things are essential to our happiness.

When balance is absent in our life we begin to feel despair and soon the best parts of ourselves, including the creativity and joy we used to know, are lost. We have all begun to feel a little bit victimized by challenges outside of our control. These feelings are created by the ultimate 'Not Me.' Even if you can identify the cause, you don't have a lot of control over the cure.

If you find yourself in a new place that feels like anything but home, or if you have spent the last few years trying to survive and have been afraid to spend anything to create a better space to live, know that you are not alone.

This is happening to millions of people. We feel overwhelmed and suddenly we begin to examine how this happened to our lives, our homes. We barely remember the childhood dreams that have vanished with the years; our self-esteem becomes corrupted by a failure not of our making. Suddenly, it feels like our potential has been bartered for security.

What do all these very big issues have to do with your home? Everything! Your home is a reflection of how you see yourself! It is the one point of beginning where you do have control and you can determine the outcome.

It is impossible to materialize anything in life that you not hold in consciousness. So, imagine, believe and achieve the desired results!

Chapter 3
To Thine Own Self, Be True

The best place to begin to learn what really appeals to you is by defining your decorating style This is the key to creating a room that really reflects the essence of you. If this sounds impossible, fear not! You can readily identify the look you crave.

1.) Look at your furniture. With a pad in hand, walk from room to room and make two truthful lists: "Love It" and "Wish I Could Replace It." Catalog everything you can, including art—just be honest. It's all based on how things make you feel.

2.) Gather the items you cherish. Check the top of your dresser, your mantel, and your bookshelves; then pull special clothes from your closet. Take a long look at the items, and make note of those that make you feel beautiful and joyful.

3.) Think about places you love and why you love them. "Picture your dream home, if you could live anywhere. How would it look? Does it have high ceilings, arches, lots of windows? Is it cozy and comfortable or sophisticated and beautiful? Then think outside of your home: "If you were invited to the Oscars, what would you wear?" This moves you beyond the limitations of your lifestyle and budget and into a new realm of creativity.

4.) Look for common threads—design, colors, shapes, materials, vibe—among the things you treasure. Note which styles pictured seem to compliment or 'match.' You may find yourself attracted to a blend of styles rather than just one. Delve into the following rooms, note which features appeal to you. This will help you translate your taste into smart decorating choices. Now let's see what your list reflects.

Sophisticated Classic

This style is an elegant blend of refined traditional furniture, jewelry-like accessories, and pale hues. Patrician old-world elements pair with cleaner Art Deco shapes. The look evokes a more formal lifestyle.

Modern Graphic/Contemporary

Modern Graphic is a fresh, fun, contemporary look that combines urban styling (imagine a downtown loft) with edgy, colorful elements and midcentury design. Simple furniture forms balance out bold accents and patterns. Think Frank Lloyd Wright combined with a Rubik's Cube.

Cozy Casual

A warm, traditional look made for relaxing with family and friends. This style draws on English and early-American furniture designs, as well as laid-back country, cottage, and farmhouse styles. Weathered, low-maintenance furnishings are easy, inviting, and built for daily life. A Norman Rockwell Painting best exemplifies this style.

Vintage Eclectic

A rich, layered look combining flea-market finds, furniture designs from various time periods, and a diverse collection of accessories and artwork. Dusty colors, timeworn or handmade textiles, and collected objects create a lived-in feel.

Victorian Styles

Luxurious, ornate and comfortable, the Victorian interior spaces bathe in nobility and class, showing off expensive fabrics and elaborate pieces of furniture. This style is what designers like to call the most luxurious, gilded design style which surprisingly is, at the same time, cozy and comfortable.

Modern Minimalist

This style is a form of extreme accuracy without heavy backgrounds. The emphasis is on simplicity, the colors may be dull or bright, in any case flashy colors. Pieces are either geometric shapes – square, rectangular, round, but the surfaces are clean, no scenery, no details.

Rustic Style

This style structure features crude, rough details, with structural elements of furniture. Lighting can be created from tree trunks, logs, branches, jute. This design is typically found in mountain vacation homes and rural areas.

Classic Reinterpreted

This is a refined style, elegant style, where classic forms details are found in a new approach. The forms preserves the structure of old forms or parts in general, updating them sometimes; or some elements of a furniture style may be combined with modern elements, creating that fusion between old and new.

Final finishing's in a new approach-painted and varnished, with different and innovative colors, surface gold, silver, finished with patina or serigraphic.

Maverick Style

The Maverick Style is a part of modern style; this approach is very inventive, unusual and unconventional. It reflects a personality that is young, explosive, and inventive and does not respect the rules. The structure can be obtained by joining pieces, or overlapping volumes and volumes. Twisting colors can be randomly chosen even for the same room, seemingly nothing happens. This is just a part of the eccentricity reflected in this style.

Contemporary

The style is really a contemporary-modern style but maintains a hot look through selected finishes and color ranges used. The finished look is a very new, modern, and cool design. Colors are balanced; warm, bright tones and pastels are out of the question when it comes to this style.

Finishes are warm, wood-veneer, solid wood doors with frames or appearance to look more polished and panels upholstered with leather sometimes. These fabrics are characteristic of this style.

High-tech

High-tech style is an innovative modern style, the emphasis being on furniture structure where every detail of combination is not random and it is part of that structure.

Screws, rivets, wheels apparent booms, rough metal finishes, appearances bulbs are specific to this style. The finishes used are often of metal, glass and plastic and wood in small proportions and for parts we find fabric-upholstered as simple as we can, leather. The colors are often dull-gray, white, small black scale.

Elegant Country

Rural style is elegant furniture style with influences from English, French or Scandinavian classic pure style can be called rural chic. Furniture finishes are nice, bright colors-white, pastel colors and forms were taking over traditional furniture but not abundant decorations. Surfaces are painted or sometimes have a slight patina.

Shabby Chic

Soft floral fabrics and accessories, pale colors, and a mix of old and new define Shabby Chic Style decor. Shabby Chic Style Furniture features time-worn, romantic styling and solid construction, making them just right for those in search of this casual, comfortable style!

Shabby Seaside

A little more sophisticated in design; the seaside shabby incorporates more substantial metals reflected in the lantern lighting, accessories and chandeliers. Think casual, polished and sleek with lightweight window treatments that billow in the breeze.

Southwestern

Southwestern interior design is characterized rich texture, earth-tone colors as the main palette (with bright accents of yellow, orange, red clay, and turquoise), hand-crafted objects, and terra cotta or clay tile roofs. Upholstery is predominantly made of woven fabrics, leather and suede's as well as animal hides. Traditional native clothing and blankets may be used as wall décor.

Wood furniture is popular and may also feature a distressed finish with metal accents. Accents can be anything from hand-painted tiles to painted ceramic pieces with roots in 16th century Mexico.

Colonial (Mid Century)

This is the style used by the first settlers to America going back to the 17th Century.

The first settlers came from England, so naturally they were very influenced by the styles of design and architecture which were around in England itself at that time. The lifestyle of the first settlers was very different from the refined and established lifestyles and towns of England.

The first settlers had to build and create everything themselves by hand so the style they used was simple and straight-forward. They made use of local building materials and techniques – which they used to create English-style designs.

Colonial decorating was rustic, basic and simple. As time went on and settlements became more refined , the style became more ornate and lavish.

Island Colonial

Today we refer to this style as 'Tommy Bahama' or Caribbean style. Alas, it sprung from the British Colonies and morphed into Island Colonial!

Especially in the colonies of the British West Indies, color palettes for walls and window treatments typically reflected the lush colors found in nature: the vivid blues of the ocean and sky; the deeper greens of tree foliage and the rich pastels of flowering plants; and the varied yellows of sand and sun. Botanical prints are common fabrics for bed benches, curtains, bedding sets and upholstered occasional chairs.

Beach Colonial

Goodness how times change! Even ten years ago we would have seen this style in a traditional home and recognized it. Not so today!

Notice the changes in today's look. White walls, white bead board on the walls and at the ceiling; it is used as trim in place of the old school crown molding! The use of very light weight fabrics hint at the ocean breeze; the use of shuttered window and door treatments permits the doors to remain open to the ocean breeze and yet keep the mosquitoes out!

Contemporary Colonial

This style feels like a contradiction but here it is! The high arched windows combined with the old pomp and circumstance found in traditional Victorian styles have now transformed into a contemporary colonial. This is reminiscent for the Italian Renaissance era!

Regardless, notice the mixture of modern sofas, traditional chairs, Victorian desks and Chrystal chandeliers to add elegance and beauty.

Chapter 4
The Color of Joy

Color is magical; it inspires, calms, soothes quietens and motivates our senses. Whether you are hoping to create a cozy, comfortable, elegant, masculine, sunny, bright or beautiful design... every room makes a statement! Like the artist beginning a new painting, treat your walls like a canvas and begin to paint a picture with color first. Paint is the least expensive method to create the greatest visual change.

Where does it start? There's a method to the madness that everyone needs to understand to successfully create the feeling you want to project.

If you simply cannot imagine what color makes you feel good, walk around in stores, model homes and your friend's homes; pay attention to each room and how it makes you feel when you walk into the space.

Each design style has colors that specifically create the look and feel of that particular style. Get familiar with how they make *you* feel. There are a multitude of shades of each of these colors, leaving you with the opportunity to personalize your design style to YOU.

Colors create inspiration!

Walk into the rooms in your home and imagine how you want them to 'feel.' Then consider the following as you make the final selection. To sum it up:

Red

Red has been shown to increase blood pressure and stimulate the adrenal glands. The stimulation of the adrenals glands helps us become strong and increases our stamina

While red has proven to be a color of vitality and ambition it has been shown to be associated with anger. Sometimes red can be useful in dispelling negative thoughts, but it can also make one irritable. Pink has the opposite effect of red.

Red is a highly energetic color. Take a look around fast food restaurants like McDonald's and you will frequently see reds and deep yellows. The

subliminal message is 'hurry up and hurry out.'
The quicker people they move, happily, through
the restaurant the more they can serve.

Pink

Pink is a lighter shade of red. It actually helps
muscles relax, inducing feelings of calm,
protection, warmth and nurturing. This color can
be used to lessen irritation and aggression as it is
connected with feelings of love. Red is sometimes
associated with sexuality, whereas pink is
associated with unselfish love.

Pink evokes a completely different feeling
even though it is a shade of red. Little girls love it
in every shade from Fuchsia to pale ice pink. It is a
feel good, warm color. I try to avoid pinks or
gender colors in master bedrooms.

Orange

Orange has proven to be a stimulus of the
sexual organs. Also, it can be beneficial to the
digestive system and can strengthen the immune
system.

It has revealed positive effects on your
emotional state. This color relieves feelings of self-
pity, lack of self-worth and unwillingness to

forgive. Orange opens your emotions and is a terrific antidepressant.

Orange is another high energy color. This color is sensual and sets a mood of sharing and playtime. The tangerine shades are warm and can be inviting in many areas. The deeper shades can actually set a sophisticated mood.

Yellow

Yellow has proven to stimulate the brain. This stimulation can make you more alert and decisive. This color makes muscles more energetic and activates the lymph system.

Similar to Orange, this is a happy and uplifting color. It can also be associated with intellectual thinking: discernment, memory, clear thinking, decision-making and good judgment. This color aids with organization and understanding of different points of view.

Yellow builds self-confidence and encourages optimism. However, a dull yellow can bring on feelings of fear. It tends to work best in kitchens where a sunny wakeup call is inviting, in bathrooms to create a light hearted feeling and in children's playrooms.

Yellow energizes; you may want to reconsider a pure yellow in children's bedrooms for that very reason.

Gold Tones

Gold tones are typically used to create a Mediterranean feel. The soft tones are warm and relaxing, the deeper ones are more calming but all work well with darker furniture tones, metals and brown accessories.

In small rooms prepare to be overwhelmed by dark gold tones. The exception to this rule is using it in half baths where accessories can create an entirely different feeling.

Green

Green is considered to be good for your heart. On a physical and emotional level, green helps your heart bring you physical equilibrium and relaxation. Green relaxes your muscles and helps to breathe deeper and slower.

The color creates feelings of comfort, laziness, relaxation and calmness. It helps us balance and soothe our emotions. Some attribute this to its connection with nature and our natural feelings of connecting with the natural world.

Gray greens

The grayer greens are very calming, allowing the accessories to make the statement and set the 'mood.'

Teals, or blue greens, lead us to a tropical paradise feeling if combined with accessories that complete that look. Think gentle ocean breezes or even tropical evening skies when considering this color.

Yet, **darker and grayer greens** can have the opposite effect. These olive green colors remind us of decay and death and can actually have a detrimental effect on physical and emotional health. Note that sickened cartoon characters always turn green.

Be careful when choosing the shade of teal for offices or places where you want to accomplish work tasks. You will probably not want to do it.

Blue

In contrast to the color red, blue proves to lower blood pressure. Blue can be linked to the throat and thyroid gland. Blue also has a very cooling and soothing affect, often making us calmer. Deep blue stimulates the pituitary gland, which then regulates sleep patterns. This deeper blue also has proved to help the skeletal structure in keeping bone marrow healthy.

We usually associate the color blue with the night and thus we feel relaxed and calmed. Lighter blues make us feel quite and away from the rush of the day. These colors can be useful in eliminating insomnia.

Like yellow, blue inspires mental control, clarity and creativity. However, too much dark blue can be depressing. In its palest shades it evokes calm and cool emotions.

Dark Blue

Dark blues, when combined with the right accessories, can be beautiful if the room is large enough to use this color for the 'canvas.' In master suites with all white accessories it becomes a paradise to relax in. Blue is the favorite color selection in all ethnic groups.

Purple

There are many shades of purple. Violet/Lavender has shown to alleviate conditions such as sunburn due to its purifying and antiseptic effect. This color also suppresses hunger and balances the body's metabolism. Indigo, a lighter purple, has been used by doctors in Texas as an anesthesia in minor operations because of its narcotic, 'a soothing or numbing agent affiliation.'

Purples have been used in the care of mental or nervous disorders because they have shown to help balance the mind and transform obsessions and fears. Indigo is often associated with the right side of the brain; stimulating intuition and imagination.

Violet

Violet is associated with bringing a sense of peace, combating shock and fear. It has a cleansing effect with emotional disturbances. This color is related to sensitivity to beauty, high ideals and stimulates creativity, spirituality and compassion. Psychic power and protection has also been associated with violet.

Purple is a warm color that evokes a feeling of royalty, velvet, and beautiful sunsets. It is a balancing color that heals and yet stimulates creativity.

Brown

Brown is the color of the earth. This color brings feelings of stability and security. Sometimes brown can also be associated with withholding emotion and retreating from the world.

This is a bold color that makes a bold statement. It has a stabilizing effect; however, the way it is used will determine the actual affect. In large rooms with light wood or white trim it can create a warm and energizing feeling.

Beige, Taupe and light neutral shades of brown are a warmer shade of white. These colors make a perfect neutral backdrop and can feel warm or impersonal depending on the way you use furnishings and accessories.

You will find that these colors will match almost any brown/beige tone furniture, settin a neutral tone.

White

White is the color of ultimate purity. This color brings feelings of peace and comfort while it dispels shock and despair.

White can be used to give you a feeling of freedom and uncluttered openness. Too much white can give feelings of separation and can be cold and instill the feeling of isolation.

It can also become the 'House of Commons!' White is cooling, calming and sometimes sophisticated; it can also feel cold, devoid of emotion and boring.

The same room transforms to sophisticated, soothing and beautiful when you add textured white window coverings, sumptuous white and contrasting rugs and throw pillows and a bold sofa. If this is combined with black and white photos you will feel like you have walked onto a movie set.

Gray

Gray is the color of independence and self-reliance, although usually associated with negativity. It can be the color of evasion and non-commitment (since it is neither black nor white.) Gray is associated with separation, lack of involvement and ultimately loneliness.

Shades of Gray

Lighter shades of gray, with white tones, work perfectly with furniture that does not have browns as a primary color. This creates a soft and cool tone in the room.

Dark Gray becomes a sophisticated backdrop when mixed with white or dark wood trim in the room.

Black

Black is a bold, dramatic, confident and sophisticated color. It is a primary color, yet the attributes of both white and gray are felt in various shades of black. It is sometimes cold. Use it sparingly unless you have a serious plan for the entire room.

Everything is crystal clear now, right? It helps to envision the room bathed in your color selection. Close your eyes and 'feel' the room, visually place your favorite furniture or accessories in the space; then select the color that delivers the message you want to project.

If this task seems impossible, check out the virtual painting resources online. All the major paint companies now offer the opportunity to upload a picture of your room, with exact lighting and issues and then change the paint color!

Painting is a task that most people can perform at some level. If you are fortunate enough to be able to afford a painter you will likely make that choice.

Many painting contractors are looking for work since the housing and new construction market has become so depressed.

This means pricing is negotiable. Don't pass on this idea until you try pricing the job unless your budget does not accommodate the possibility.

If you intend to paint the rooms yourself (I always have) there are a few tips that will make your project run smoothly and produce results you can be proud of.

a) Choose a good, dependable paint. Satin or eggshell paint creates a soft and nearly flat appearance that does not show defects in the wall.

This happens because it has no sheen; light does not reflect off of it. Keep that in mind when choosing the color, you may want to slightly lighten the shade.

The washable flat paint also hides imperfections and works nicely with the Shabby Chic look. It is a little more expensive so weigh the benefits against the cost and then decide what works best for your budget.

b) Cover the floors, even if you think they are easy to clean or not really important. You'll be glad you did when clean up time is upon you.

c) If you are not completely comfortable with your trim brush, tape, tape and tape again.

d) Buy good paint rollers and the right length of roller covers. You really do get what you pay for in the paint materials.

e) Great brushes (horsehair if possible, with thin tapered edges) are the easiest to get a perfect edge on the trim work.

I was given the opportunity to learn from a professional and discovered that taking a long look at the angle of the wall and where it meets the ceiling is vital to know which way to set the brush on the wall and trim it out.

Stand back and take a good look at the angles of the walls and the ceiling and set the brush down with the bare tip of the brush at the point where the wall meets the ceiling.

f) Roll the walls in (W) patterns and back again. This is one time when straight lines will not be your friend. The more directions you roll in, the smoother the overall finish will be.

g) Use enamel paint on trim work. It wears beautifully and washes easily. It is also a pain to work with as it is almost never washable and turpentine will become a new friend.

h) I try to avoid semi gloss finishes. They are dated, show every imperfection on the walls and attract attention to the walls rather than letting them be the canvas they should be.

Who knew there was so much emotion in a simple can of paint? Make your selection and be brave; the results are so worth the effort.

If you are renting, get permission to paint and be prepared to repaint the walls to white when you leave.

Painting Your Room

For step-by-step guides to painting your rooms I highly recommend going to your favorite search engine and selecting one of a host of available sites that provide written and video instructions.

The basic rules are light colors in rooms where the natural light is limited, thereby causing the room to feel dark when you enter it and light ceilings unless you have very high or vaulted ceilings. If you have chosen to paint your ceilings a different color, chose one this is a lighter shade of your original choice if you have low ceilings.

I have to add one more really neat tip I learned from a professional painter. I lived in a home with 19' ceilings; some were vaulted, some were trey. All seemed pretty daunting to me! I paid the painter for one room and learned very quickly the best tips I have ever been given.

Invest in the best paintbrush you can afford to buy. It should be very soft, horsehair if possible, thin and tapered at the tip and sturdy.

Trimming paint is all about the angle. Stand back for a moment and really look at the angle in the room.

You paint trim beginning from the back of the brush, allowing the tip of the brush (the pointed tapered end) to drag behind the paint stroke and fill in. The tip should find the 'bead' in the wall where the ceiling and wall come together.

Make SURE that you add the paint to the side of the brush that will be on the wall, wiping off excess paint on the opposite side of the brush.

Stand back once the paint is on the brush and look again at the ANGLE of the wall. Then, lay the paint brush flat against the wall, beginning at the back of the brush and drag along the line in a smooth motion.

I just finished painting the color 'Peppercorn' on a wall against a white ceiling and white baseboards with no taping or preparation and the line is perfect – simply by using this method! Try it first; it is a time saver and money saver.

Painting Your Floors

This is a very simple procedure to complete; however, the most important issue with painting floors is making the determination that the floor is suitable for painting or, what you need to do to prepare it before you start. It must be smooth and moisture free. Wood floors can be sanded and any spaces filled in with wood filler. Concrete must be free of cracks or blemished or be repaired to have a smooth working surface.

Once your floor is properly prepared you will need to select your color and ask your paint supplier to mix it from the floor painting bases. It is applied with a roller using an extension. Two coats are the minimal you will want to apply. Then finish with poly to protect the paint and give the floor a lasting sheen.

The internet is a wonderful place to learn anything today. Go back to your favorite search engine and find the particular problem you are facing. You will be sure to find detailed instructions and probably even videos to walk you through the process.

Wallpapering Instructions

Wallpapering a wall or a room may feel a little scary if you've never attempted it. The good news is that it is a fairly simple process. Just as in painting a wall, preparing the surface is the most is very important first step. If your walls are not smooth this will be obvious even with the wallpaper.

You will need to patch and sand any holes or cracks on the surface. If your walls have really obvious defects you can sand the area first and cut a piece of a brown paper bag to cover the area; use your wallpaper glue to attach the paper to the wall.

Press it firmly into place and smooth out the wrinkles and let it dry. You will have a smooth surface that easily covers with the new paper.

Chapter 5
Here's Looking At You

You guessed it; it's time for windows and how to treat them to compliment your plan.

You can create the design style you have chosen; however, the windows are important to arrive at creating the look you are planning.

Take a good look at your windows and the placement of them. This is the not the time to decide whether they need replaced; we simply want to use them to the best advantage for your design style. Windows are square, paned, arched, long and narrow, wide and short, they come in a multitude of sizes and shapes.

Regardless of your window style, we need to get to know them.

Window Styles

Windows reflect every structural style. They can be high/short/narrow or Dormer style. High arched window, long and narrow windows Abundance of narrow windows, high, arched windows, and cornered windows.

Add to these traditional styles, the round room with a wall of windows, and those narrow tall windows with arch above. And we've all had those high, standard square windows and sliding glass doors take the place of windows.

Window panes are a part of the construction in older windows; if you don't like them you have a few choices. You can use a window treatment that obscures the design or replace them.

The newer paned windows are strips that will snap out and give you a clean un-obscured window if that look is attractive to you.

This book is not about replacing windows but that is an option if you desire to do so! We are going to work with what we have.

Some window styles reflect the style of the home. For instance, a home with arched windows may be somewhat of a challenge when creating a Primitive Design. Still, we can do that. Just keep reading!

Likewise, the older more typical square windows challenge the Contemporary, Spanish and Southwestern designs.

Once you have selected your style, paint colors and floor treatment, the windows complete your canvas. The picture will be complete when the room is finished!

Tips to begin:

a) Wash the windows!

b) Clean the woodwork and paint if necessary.

c) Assess the challenge! Do the size and style of the windows work as they are, or do you need to change the perception to create your style?

d) Get creative; packaged window treatments are made for the 'house of commons,' not your palace! When creating your own design, you become the leader, not the follower.

e) Measure the actual windows both vertical and horizontal; then measure from the top of the wall to the floor.

f) Take a moment and caulk your windows. Heat and air conditioning is lost through windows and doors, increasing your energy bills and making it harder to heat or cool your home. Caulking also prevents ants and other undesirables from entering your home.

g) If you live in a manufactured house, tear down those 'made for a trailer' window treatments! Nothing says I'm perched on wheels like the little valances and kitchen curtains hanging all over the house. You will be amazed at how your home can look!

Now we're ready to begin! Let's look at materials, and what is possible.

If you are working with Southwestern, Spanish or Primitive designs, regardless of whether you have square, arched or small windows; try picking up full length wood bi-fold doors and painting them or grab a can of Min Wax spray stain and put the finish of your choice on the doors. They fold out just like shutters and can be used on sliders as well as windows.

For very little money you have custom window treatments!

Cottage designs work great with the plantation shutter styles. You can hang these higher and wider that the actual window if you need to visually increase the size of the window to make a bigger statement.

Give some thought to hand railing for stairs and how they can work as curtain rods! These come in nearly every style, some with intricate design in addition to the more typical styles.

Mediterranean and Spanish styles can use wrought iron pieces to create interesting rods.

We're creating a masterpiece here and can hardly be bothered to simply pick up a simple rod and hang it up. Window design starts from the rods.

If your home has small, older windows try hanging your drapes from the top of the wall and extend them out past the actual window. Visually the wall and the windows appear larger; and the room feels more substantial. This is also a good trick to eliminate the arches if your design is more suited to a straight line in the windows.

Check out the remnant section of the fabric store. Look for large bolts that are offered at $1.00 a yard. You're looking for texture that will compliment your personal style.

If you're not handy with a sewing machine, never fear; purchase Stitch Witchery and head for your ironing board to create rod pockets at the top and finished hems at the bottom.

Curtains that pool onto the floor are much more appealing and do not look like pre-packaged curtains.

Look at sheets if you do not want to spend time at the fabric store. They are long, offered in a wide range of colors and already have top and bottom hems.

Just slit the sides of the top hem and insert the rod after using your stitch witchery magic or hand needle and thread to complete the newly cut seam.

Sheets work great as shower curtains on spring rods; insert a liner behind it and decorate away!

If you plan to tie your curtains back look at wide cloth ribbon or rope; trims that are not so fussy and do not appear prepackaged.

If you are working with a Victorian, Classic or Traditional design look at the long table cloths that also offer special designs particular to your style. Try adding long strings of pearls that are found in craft stores and Christmas decorations. They make fabulous trims!

Natural hemp ropes work perfectly as tiebacks for Cottage (especially Seaside Cottage designs) Country and Primitive.

Look for natural fabrics like unbleached muslin to bring a true country or Primitive feeling into the space.

If you have typical windows and are looking for a whole new look with an unconditional fix; define your style and consider adding plantation shutters that are 18" shy of the top of the window.

Add leaded glass or faux lead stained Plexiglas sections; place this section above the shutter to cover the rest of the window and add a trim board.

Suddenly your 'same old windows' now feature leaded glass and thick, rich wood shutters.

Stain or paint the shutters to match your design plan.

You no longer have average or typical windows. It's a brand new view!

Avoid those 'found in every home' mini blinds if possible. They feel like a cheap fix, and are unbecoming to a palace and your plan. Dare to be different!

Discard the 'fan' treatment for the top of arched windows. The arches grace the top of the window; leave them bare and let the sun shine in!

Part of your plan is to make your home different and spectacular; affordably!

Make a real effort to think outside the traditional prepackaged window treatments available almost everywhere. Search for great deals on things that can be repurposed into your plan.

For the classic window covering look, nothing compares to custom fabric drapes and curtains. The simplicity of hanging drapery adds elegance and sophistication to your dining room, living room, or bedroom. Drapes hang from above the window down to the floor, hanging on either a rod or with pins and a pin knuckle for easy sliding.

And because custom drapes are long and made of fabric, you can get them in just about any color you can imagine. Not only do they give your rooms a classy look, they can also be matched to your decor easily and precisely.

What's best - Pleats or No Pleats?

Pleated drapes are designed to create a consistent pleated look starting at the top where the gathers form. The drapes then hang in lines, giving a long, tall look to any room. With pins and a pin knuckle, you'll find that pleated drapes look perfect all the time. The shape and frequency of the pleats will be consistent, no matter whether the drapes are open or closed.

Drapes that don't have pleats will have a flat and straight look with wider folds when the drapes are pulled closed. Flat drapes are usually hung on a bar, either with large grommet holes or with simple fabric loops. Un-pleated custom drapes look great in dark colors, such as you might want in your bedroom or entertainment den.

Colors, Stripes and Solids

Custom drapes come in a wide assortment of colors, including stripes, solids, and even textures like linen and a crushed look like linen.

This means that you can match your colors as well as an appropriate texture to your rooms.

Lining Options

Some drapes do not require lining to block the light. But if you want something lightweight with a liner, you also have the option of pleated or not pleated liners, which will aid in darkening the room and keeping the ambient temperature even.

Window Treatments

Long Panes

Bare windows are rarely the best choice when decorating a room. Window treatments--whether piped, pleated, puddled, or plain--add fluidity and softness to a room's hard edges. And in terms of practicality, they add privacy and light control. They also can help conceal a room's flaws or accentuate its charms.

Three of design's heavy hitters--fabric, texture, and pattern--come into play when you're selecting the perfect treatment. But choosing the type of treatment your room needs is the first order of business. We've made it easy: These timeless treatments will inspire and guide you through the looks that stylish windows are wearing.

Puddled Curtains

Puddled curtains are an exception to the "just touching the floor." rule. Puddled curtains are several inches too long. Puddled curtains have a luxurious look that is often preferred by homeowners who have formally decorated and furnished homes. Puddled curtains work best when they are stationary, meaning that you do not need to open and close them often. They also look best when they are made from luxurious fabrics and are placed in formal settings.

Valances

A valance is a little bit of fabric that does a big job. It hangs across the top of a window, adding softness, color, and pattern to a hard architectural element. Purely decorative, a valance helps establish a room's style. At its most basic, a slip of fabric can be attached to a rod with clip rings. For more detail, add pinch pleats.

The simple valance is a casual treatment that works well for family areas such as the kitchen, breakfast room, and bathroom. In rooms where privacy isn't an issue, the valance can hang alone.

When privacy is a concern, the valance easily pairs with a hard treatment, such as a blind, shade, or shutters.

Box-Pleated Valances

Those who appreciate a classic decorating style will fall in love with the box-pleated valance. This tailored treatment is a natural in rooms where you want a formal air, such as a living room, dining room, or master bedroom. The stationary treatment's crisp stitched pleats lie flat against a mounting board, which is typically attached to the wall with simple L-shape brackets.

Simple Swags

Sometimes a simply knotted scarf worn around the neck is the perfect accent for an outfit. A simple swag on a window dresses up a room the same way. A loosely slung fabric strip, unlined or lined, draped over a decorative rod or wound over a tieback at each top corner of a window frame can add an abundance of style. The middle of the fabric strip acts as a valance; the ends, whether cut into opposing diagonals or simply hemmed, softly hang down the sides of the window.

Swags can be made of luxurious fabrics to fit formal decor or dressed down in cottons befitting a cottage or country home. The beauty of this style is its simplicity, so it's most appropriate used alone on windows where privacy is not an issue.

Balloon Shades

For the ultimate romantic gesture, nothing beats a billowy balloon shade. This sumptuous fabric shade features cascading scallops that culminate in graceful, blousy folds along the bottom. Cords strung though rings on the back make the shade movable, and as the treatment is raised, the vertical gathers create dramatic poufs. Because this treatment usually remains raised, it acts as a valance more often than a shade.

The amount of fabric used--at least twice the width of the window--creates the opulent look. Large designs can get lost in the multiple gathers, so opt for solid-color or small-pattern fabrics. Be aware, too, that the number of gathers, pleats, or scallops creates different looks within the balloon-shade and valance family. An Austrian shade, for example, has less shirring and is therefore more tailored than its cousin, the balloon shade. Because this window treatment is so showy, use it in small doses.

Tie-Up Shade

Simplicity is the name of the game with tie-up shades. Sometimes called a stagecoach-style shade, this economical treatment uses fabric in its most unconstructed form: It hangs flat from a rod or mounting board, and then the bottom edge is hand-rolled or folded to the desired position.

Fabric ties, ribbons, or cords hold the rolls or folds in place. Adjusting the shade requires untying and rerolling it by hand, making this treatment more decorative than functional. Consider using it where you're likely to leave the shade down to hide an unsightly view or open in a room where privacy or sunlight isn't an issue.

Tie-up Shade Tips

Because so much of the fabric is visible, a tie-up shade offers a good opportunity to use a large-scale pattern. Just make sure the fabric keeps its shape when rolled. Or add bulk by lining a lightweight fabric to give the shade a finished look when rolled up. For tidy rolls, sew a dowel into the bottom hem. This treatment's simple styling makes it a natural for casual decorating schemes, but it also can be a welcome change of pace in formal rooms.

Roman Shades

For the look of luxury without yards of flowing fabric, a Roman shade is a wise choice. When closed, the shade is a flat fabric panel. When raised, cascades of deep, horizontal folds are responsible for the tidy look. Cords strung through rings on the back of the fabric give the shade its mobility. Some Roman shades are made without dowels or lining, resulting in looser, puffier folds.

Roman Shade Tips

A Roman shade can be mounted inside or outside a window frame. Though the shade is often used alone, it can be the practical layer combined with side panels or a valance. Appropriate almost anywhere, a Roman shade's level of formality is defined by fabric and trim choices. You could use plain muslin in a sunroom or toile in a master bedroom. Just be sure to choose fabric that can form handsome folds.

Cornices

Think of a cornice as a wood valance, it is typically made from plywood, assembled with wood screws and corner brackets, then painted or covered with wallpaper or fabric and mounted to the wall above a window. Like a valance, a cornice can appear alone or team with another treatment. Because it is usually made of wood, a cornice benefits from being paired with a soft treatment, such as a curtain or fabric shade, to temper its hard lines.

These structural lines are especially effective in rooms that lack interesting architecture. They can camouflage a window's wimpy trim or bring interest to a room that doesn't have crown moldings.

Rod-Pocket Drapes

Of the many ways to attach a drapery panel to a rod, few match the ease of the rod pocket. In this treatment, the curtain rod simply slips through a channel sewn into the panel's top edge. The tighter the fit, the more dramatic the shirring effect produced. For a ruffled header, sew a pocket a few inches down from the top edge; when the rod is pushed through, the fabric above it fans out to form a ruffle.

Rod-pocket panels are commonly made of lightweight fabrics and left unlined for a casual look. But don't overlook this style for more formal decor. For a sumptuous style statement, consider plush velvet panels shirred tightly on a substantial rod.

Because panels don't slide easily on a rod, especially when tightly gathered, they're typically used in the closed position or held open with decorative tiebacks.

Panels with Rings

Prickly metal hooks used to be standard fare for hanging draperies. Stuck into the back of a panel, the hardware was out of sight and out of mind. No more. Wood or metal rings that slide along a pole allow you to put hardware in a starring role, complementing virtually any style of drapery. Besides being fashionable, panels with rings are easy to open and close and offer an alternative to anyone who dislikes the cord-and-pulley system of traverse rods.

Pleated Panels

In the world of window treatments, pleated drapery panels are the classics. They withstand the whims of window fashion, adding elegance and sophistication to any room. There are several styles of pleats, all of which are sewn into a panel's top edge to create a decorative header. Pleats are often formed with the help of header tape, which is available by the yard at fabrics stores. Sewn to the panel's back, the tape forms pleats when pulled. Hooks are then inserted into the tape and hung on rings, or more typically traverse rods, which have a cord-and-pulley system for opening and closing the panels.

Shutters

Wood Plantation Shutters Add Enduring, Classic Beauty to Your Home

The most desired of all window coverings are real wood shutters. A classic window covering choice, they exude a sense of permanence, so every time you see them, you know that you are indeed home.

Real wood shutters are made from 100% North American Hardwoods, which have been harvested from certified forests. Shutters are available in a variety of finishes to complement your decor. Slat sizes are also a matter of choice. Choose from 2" slats, 3" slats or view-preserving 4" slats.

Curtain and Drapery Lengths

Floor Length Curtains

Just as pants that are several inches too short are unflattering and distracting, so are curtains that are too short. Curtains that hang about 1/8 to 1/4 inch above the floor, just touching the floor or have a slight break look neat and professional. Decorators often hang curtains so that they are as close to the ceiling as possible, to make windows and ceilings look taller. This is good advice, so do hang your curtains as high as possible, but not so high that they do not touch the floor.

Puddled Curtains

Puddled curtains are an exception to the "just touching the floor rule. Puddled curtains are several inches too long. Puddled curtains have a luxurious look that is often preferred by homeowners who have formally decorated and furnished homes. Puddled curtains work best when they are stationary, meaning that you do not need to open and close them often. They also look best when they are made from luxurious fabrics and are placed in formal settings.

Window-length Curtains

You may choose to dress shorter windows with shorter curtains. Short windows that do not extend close to the floor are often found in bathrooms and kitchens. If your window is closer to the ceiling than the floor, it can look awkward to have floor-length curtains. Instead, hang or hem your curtains so that the bottom of the panel is either just touching the window sill, or hanging to the bottom of the trim underneath the window.

Standard Ready-made Curtain Lengths

The height of your home's ceilings often determines the length of your curtain panels, as builders usually install taller windows in homes with higher ceilings. Ready-made curtains generally come in standard lengths: 84 inches for 8-foot ceilings, 96 inches for 9-foot ceilings and 108 inches for 10-foot ceilings. If you like to puddle your curtains, simply buy one size up. You can sometimes find curtains that are 120 inches long; these work well for puddling curtains in a home with 10-foot ceilings.

Final Considerations

When you hang your ready-made curtains, always measure them first. Dimensions listed on the curtain packages are approximate, and the actual curtain may be slightly longer or shorter than the package states. Take any curtain rings or headers into consideration, as these can add or take length away from curtain measurements.

Chapter 6
A Path Well Lit

Light always follows the path of the beautiful.
~ Unknown

What's YOUR 'feel good' style? You are likely to find it in your lighting selections! This may surprise you but; the light choices you make typically define your style.

Lighting is everything! Choose wisely and you will be well on your way to creating YOUR space. If you are uncertain as to what your style actually is take a look at the lighting examples in this chapter.

Notice what you are drawn to and then explore that look. You will probably find that some of your furniture pieces will work nicely to create that style, the other pieces we will work on!

If you discover that you are drawn to a particular style of lighting, you will probably discover that is your style! Some are combined styles that work well together to create a specific look and feel.

Great lighting is found in yard sales, online stores, (Overstocked.com is a good one) eBay, and on Craig's List (many contractors sell lighting that customers rejected on Craig's List), in the newspaper, at thrift stores and, especially at the Habitat for Humanity Thrift Store!

Habitat for Humanity has been very blessed to receive donations from Lowes, Home Depot and a host of other large companies. If you have one locally, find it and bookmark it in your mind!

At the end of this chapter you will find detailed instructions on installing your lighting. If you are not comfortable with doing this job, look in the newspaper, on Craig's List or a weekly paper that has Handyman advertisements or ask a neighbor or relative to do this.

The job is relatively simple so long as you are simply replacing a fixture. On the other hand, if you are relocating electrical fixtures, call a licensed electrician to complete this for you. This is an added expense and we will explore ways to sue what you have and work from that point.

If you take a moment to carefully review the styles you will notice that each has lines, shapes and detail that are particular to the style.

Find the one that you like the most things about the look and feel, imagine them in your own home and you will have defined your own personal style!

Some tips about lighting your palace:

1) Entry areas greet everyone; choose a size in your style that is befitting of the greeting and the size of the area you are defining.

2) Long entry halls may require a larger light and wall sconces or an entry table with lamps to properly light the area.

3) Don't select long, pendant lighting for the entry if you have 8' ceilings. You can do this in the dining area because the table is placed under the lighting and no one is walking in the area.

4) Grand foyers deserve a grand light! Go big or go home.

5) Wall sconces around mirrors in bath areas are welcoming and provided necessary dressing light.

6) Choose your dining room light in proportion with the size of your table. Don't be afraid to drop it lower than what you might think is typical. Lighting makes a statement! If you want it to be intimate lighting you have to set the stage with furniture and accessories and say it with light!

7) Avoid fans on dining room lighting unless you want to create a very informal space. It also cools the food on the table and stirs dust above and onto the food.

8) Ceiling fans are a must in some areas; although some decorators rush to remove them, others will scurry to install them! If you determine that a ceiling fan must be in your bedrooms, avoid the inexpensive (and cheap looking) light kits; opt for nice lamps and a decorative fan that matches the room decor.

9) If you have a budget that permits you to shop for quality fans with lighting that makes a difference in the room, go for it!

10) Breakfast bars in kitchens become a special place if they are defined with two or three pendant lights.

11) Hall lighting is largely ignored, yet it is typically a long, dark area that provides entry into probably half of your home. Use that opportunity to make a special statement!

Track lighting works nicely in long narrow walkways. It is now available in attractive styles that fit any décor. You may want to look at those as an option, or, supplement your overhead lights with recessed lights for low ceilings or wall sconces.

Now you are now ready for the final piece in building your canvas, the flooring. This is the really fun part as you begin setting the stage for the furniture and your new look. You are on the way to discovering the creative giant within!

Chapter 7
Ushering In Your Luck

"Opportunity dances with those already on the dance floor."

~ H. Jackson Brown Jr.

Floors are important! They are the entry to and the roadway that carries the traffic through your home. Who knew! After spending all that time on painting and properly defining your home with perfect lighting; there's the same old floor! Now what?

I think energy is very important in our lives. We can 'feel' it but may not be aware of how it affects us.

Ensuring that your home is in harmony with nature and your immediate environment will affect every person who enters your home is a positive way.

The greater the imbalance, the more intense its effect on the occupants; this kind of imbalance distorted energy fields as these fields begin to resonate to give rise to hazardous levels of radiation which affect the occupants of the home.

Ignoring this will interrupt the smooth flow of energy in and around your home. Learning the principals of Feng Shui will help to restore the imbalance or equalizing the thermal difference.

Some excellent ideas to remember as you correct energy imbalance in your home are:

•   More open spaces in the North and East direction.
•   Solid walls and no openings on the South side.
•   Adding more greenery or trees in the South to have a humid environment.
•   But, most importantly, choose good flooring.

The flooring in a building not only breathes life in terms of décor and aesthetics but also defines how the energy flows there and through the space.

You can control the atmosphere of your house or

apartment. Big surface areas such as flooring will have the greatest influence, and it is worth taking great care over the materials you use.

Natural materials create the best energy flow. These include wood, brick marble, granite and slate. Marble has never been out of fashion and is available in a variety of colors. Bricks are available in different shades of red and orange can also be used as ethnic flooring. Bamboo flooring has recently become very fashionable and is eco friendly because it reproduces so quickly.

Natural materials tend to carry energy more easily than synthetic materials.

A rough textured surface (such as a wool carpet) slows down chi, making it more yen. Hard or shiny surfaces (such as ceramic tiles) speed up the flow of chi, creating a more yang atmosphere. By incorporating these guidelines into your flooring plan you are able to harmonize the energy in the room and around your family and guests.

Every natural material enhances a specific flow of chi; applying the simplicity of the eight directions; you can determine which materials are best suited to each area of your home.

Using specific materials will lead to a more harmonious exchange of chi and develop distinct atmospheres in each part of your home. Review the list below and apply the ideas to your home and the atmosphere and energy flow you wish to create.

• White marble which enhances positive energy and reflects and polarizes sunlight well in the Northeast sector.

• Shades of yellow, like the popular Southwest Indian Yellows towards the Southwest promote good energy flow. The Southwest is designated the negative energy corner so brighter colors that anchor the space and create a 'heavy' energy attraction correct this.

• The Northwest sections of your home are influenced by wind energy. Choose blues, whites, silvers and creams that reflect the flow of the wind.

• The southeast corner of your home will do well with reds and oranges in some shade that fits your color plan.

Floors will shout or whisper, depending on how you treat them. Some styles seem to feel like they must be defined by specific flooring. That is the shouting method!

If your floors do not 'match' your idea of the design you are creating you have a few choices to make them whisper so the bulk of your masterpiece will shout.

If you live in an apartment or a rental home you may think you are stuck with your floors; take heart.

Solutions for floor shouters:

Cover the floor! That's right; cover it with something that ties it to the style you are creating. Even if the floor has carpet, cover it with a large room size rug or one that leaves only a border of the original color, if there is anything you like about it.

I urge you to check out Flea Markets, Thrift Stores, Consignment Stores, Craig's List and Overstocked.com to find a rug that will make the cut.

b) Select the very inexpensive woven mats to create an oriental feeling in the space.

c) Tile and carpet squares are sold by the box pretty inexpensively. Find the nap and color that you work for your idea and put them in place.

d) If you own your home, have carpet and cannot afford to replace it with anything; take it up and paint the subflooring! It works great with rugs to complete the design.

e) If you have wood floors that are the wrong color or in a bad state of repair; make the repairs and rent a floor sander.

Sanding is a fairly easy job that provides you with a clean slate. Then select the stain that makes you want to shout about it!

f) Barter the work with someone who has materials and experience.

g) Create visual points to break an open floor plan by changing the flooring. In very open plans the entry can break away from tile or something durable to wood or carpet in the actual living space, thereby creating a defined space without walls.

h) Avoid the 'checkerboard' floor syndrome. Breaking the flooring is fine for obvious areas like entry's, kitchens, baths and lanais. A different floor color or style in every room dates your home and makes it look and feel choppy and smaller.

When flooring changes design, color or material in every room you will soon begin to feel like you've been check-mated instead of mated with your dream home!

Kicking your old floor to the curb?

Consider other options. If you have always wanted wood floors and they are not practical for your home or location; search out the new laminate and tile selections that mimic wood.

'Looks like wood' tile floors

Tile manufactures have listened to their buying audience and created beautiful tiles that look like wood. It is easy care, scuff proof and humidity does not affect its performance.

Save diagonal ceramic or marble tile jobs for large rooms. While they are beautiful, they also attract attention to the floor space and make the room appear smaller.

Select light tile colors to make your room appear larger. Larger tile sizes also make the room appear more spacious.

Pergo or other manufactured wood flooring is far less expensive but also, far less durable. It is manmade wood and a little easier to install but have a care here, if it is not properly adhered to the subflooring, it 'bounces' when you walk across it and screams 'thrift.'

Real hard wood is more expensive but if time is on your side you can watch for the spring specials and the dead of winter liquidation of these materials.

Carpeting is still considered a good option for bedrooms and upper levels. It is available in a multitude of styles, naps, colors and designs.

Unless you plan to live forever in your home, or don't mind repainting later, avoid fads and colors that you will tire of. Select colors that you can interchange accessories with to create a new look and feel later.

The general rule with carpeting is Berbers are more durable, neutrals are preferable.

Lose the notion that a carpeted kitchen, bath or dining room is a good idea. Most people prefer to be able to easily clean the surfaces of these areas.

In homes that offer large, separate dining areas this rule can be bent; personally, I'd rather not; opt for wood or tile.

When you begin to install flooring, doors, hardware or plumbing you must decide whether you are handy and want to learn or tackle these tasks alone or, whether it is time to search the kingdom for qualified and affordable assistance.

Chapter 8
A Change is Gonna Come!

A lot of topics have been covered in the process of building your 'canvas, a visual image of your new space. This is an important process, necessary to determine exactly what you want to create and which of the ideas fit into your budget and final plan for the space you want to transform. Soon we will review different rooms in the home and how these ideas can work, very affordably, to create a stunning completed project.

For now, it is time to take a look at how to make it happen. While pictures may speak a thousand words, definitions make it a lot easier to arrive at your desired look and feel

Cozy Casual

Plush upholstery, often slip covered, with roll or square arms and skirts or ball feet.

Indestructible tables with turned legs, trestles, or substantial pedestal bases define this style. Think warm wood tones with rustic or distressed finishes and natural fabrics, like cotton and wool; these fabrics work beautifully with Cozy Casual design styles.

Solid textiles, simple stripes, or unfussy floral patterns in muted colors complete this look.

Vintage Eclectic

A rich, layered look combining flea-market finds, furniture designs from various time periods (including Victorian pieces and 18th-century French styles), and a diverse collection of accessories and artwork. Dusty colors, timeworn or handmade textiles, and collected objects create a lived-in feel. Think Paris flea markets, Granny's teacups, the film Grey Gardens.

Jewel tones mixed with washed-out, chalky shades; Antique and vintage elements interspersed with newer, offbeat items.

A varied mix of fabrics (on pillows, upholstery, and window treatments), including jacquards, paisleys, ethnic tapestries, folk motifs, botanicals, and floral designs, Crystal chandeliers and embellished lamps; Abundant art and decorative accents on walls and surfaces.

Older homes lend themselves to the vintage look and feel architecturally. Wallpaper is used in abundance to create this style. Flocked wallpaper particularly lends itself to this design but the beauty of vintage eclectic is the word eclectic. It allows you to use anything you to create a cozy inviting environment with a plan! This creates an artsy environment that is cozy, comfortable and beautiful.

Low ceilings, lack of natural lighting, boxy architectural design, and baseboard heating and worn carpet make this feel impossible.

While wood flooring is more suited to this style, let's assume that you are stuck with this flooring because it is a rental or new flooring is not in the budget.

When you have low ceilings combined with a lack of natural lighting you have to address those issue with the walls and flooring. We have beige carpeting here so the examples being shown reflect this shade. You can do the same when making your choices based on what you currently have if you are going to keep it.

Something light that draws our attention up will make the room feel bigger and the ceilings feel higher.

If you're not wallpapering because it is a rental, because the budget does not work with wallpapering or maybe you simply hate wallpaper or have heard horror stories about removing it, let's paint instead!

In this illustration we have low ceilings and a lack of lighting. This commands light paint. You can use nearly any shade in the eclectic theme. Just pick the lighter hues to allow the room to visually 'grow.' Stay with one paint color in the room and avoid accent colors in a darker shade. It will only break the travel of the eye and make it feel smaller.

If possible, convert your baseboards to bright white. A low ceiling demands bright white paint to 'lift' it up.

If you have the cut out area shown in this photo, referred to as a pass through from kitchen to dining rooms, it is time to make it disappear.

While we were only addressing the opening in this room, these curtains all come in lengths of 84 inches. You can easily cut them to the desired length. Let's leave them all the way to the floor and lose the exposed baseboard for no extra expense.

If you don't have anything you need to 'hide' you can buy the least expensive, which will be the shortest, and then cut them to fit just below the opening or whatever length is desirable to you.

This style loves the old 'early junk' collection of furniture! Yard sales, garage sales, thrift stores, Craig's List and a multitude of other places will provide any accessory you are missing. Mix, mix and mix some more.

If you are stuck with carpeting you hate, clean it and then add rugs you find in thrift stores.

Modern mirrors or ornate older ones work equally well. Paint them in metallic or complimentary colors and just be YOU!

Victorian Styles

Interior spaces are bathed in nobility and class, showing off expensive fabrics and elaborate pieces of furniture. Victorian is what designers like to call the most luxurious, gilded design style which surprisingly is, at the same time, cozy and comfortable.

With its name and origins drawn from the Victorian Age (period named after the reign of Queen Victoria), this lavish and sophisticated style develops royal features, residing in the excessive use of furniture, fabrics, patterns, floral motifs and other accessories.

Architectural components such as coving arches, cornicing and ceilings are considered key elements in obtaining the Victorian aspect. You can easily turn your plain room surfaces into Victorian masterpieces with specific decorative details like bas-reliefs with nature motifs, carvings and moldings.

Because Victorian relies on ornate wall coverings, rich, full window treatments and lots of 'stuff,' you can pretty much make this style work in any architectural design.

If you live in a traditionally designed home you need only choose the perfect paint or wallpaper color to compliment your color scheme and change out the lighting. This design style is all about the accessories, wall hangings, lighting, furniture and drapery, lots of it! The Victorian era of furniture and accessories is abundant in thrift stores and on line.

If your home has the typical 4 inch baseboards try adding an additional trim piece. You can buy these, prefinished and very ornate, at Lowes or Home Depot very inexpensively. Pick up the contractor glue while you are there and make this really easy!

Be creative! If you have furniture that looks nothing at all like this and you are stuck with using it then add complimentary throw pillows that do reflect this era. You can sand the wood pieces lightly and apply dark cherry or mahogany Minwax and create a totally different look to the pieces. No fear!

Look for ornate lighting, candles, trays and massive mirrors and just go with the flow. The window treatments are vital here. Look for deals on velvet or velvet look-alike drapes or satin drapes. If you love your very plain drapes but they won't work pick up complimentary colored tousles at the fabric store and some stitch witchery. You can pick up tasseled trim for the lamp shades and use fabric glue to bring them into this era. In minutes you will have transformed your old contemporary drapes into beautiful Victorian drapes. This same works to create matching pillow for the sofas.

Flocked wallpaper is the best choice for this design plan. The typical colors range from burgundy to a rich cream color and soft white with lots of gold in the accent pieces. Royal blue was frequently used as an accent color in this era.

For accessories, pick up gold or bronze spray paint and re-purpose your lamps, picture shades and mirrors to create the Victorian look.

Wooden floors are the best option to easily transform a traditional space to Victorian. If you don't have them and can't get them, try to locate a room size rug. These are in abundant supply and are inexpensive. Try to stay within your color scheme as you search for gold's, burgundies, royal blue and cream colors to set the stage for flooring.

In newer homes this transformation will likely require all the walls to be wallpapered. I suggest white trim; the final trims are what make the Victorian statement.

If you have the funds (not a lot) you can buy the plastic insulated trim and apply to the windows to create beautiful paned windows.

In a room that has commercial grade Berber carpeting I think you would be well advised to pull it up and simply paint the floor if you are not able to install wood flooring now. Whether your subflooring is concrete or wood, it will paint nicely if you sand off the high spots and apply 2-3 coats and then add a coat of poly to keep the shine. Then add large rungs to complete the cool.

If you have track lighting in the center of the room where you would typically find a chandelier, replace it with a chandelier.

Budget permitting you can add prefinished molding to the baseboards to increase the size and also as crown molding. This was detailed in the early part of the Victorian discussion.

The furniture detail is the same as in earlier part of this chapter. Do not be afraid to use spray paint on your accessories, frames and furniture. Metal tones are available very inexpensively. For lamps, paint them and then just change the shade to a one with a Victorian look.

Don't shy away from thrift stores and auctions to find the extra accessories or furnishings you are missing. Auctions are shamefully inexpensive on Victorian furniture and accessories.

Very inexpensive pedestals are a wonderful way to bring in the charm of the Victorian era without blowing the budget. Pick up two and add a random piece of glass for a great entry or sofa table. Single pedestals hold decorative bust's and look beautiful and very elegant.

Tips: Try painting tables in the room gold; then add marbleized spray paint for the top! Make sure you add poly to create the 'marble' shine.

Discarded 6 panel doors are a perfect 'paneled screen'. Collect them at Habitat for Humanity or on Craig's List and paint or stain. Connect with hinges and you now have a wood paneled wall!

Add ceiling medallions to showcase a chandelier or important lighting component. These are available in white, gold, bronze and a multitude of colors. If you want to create something unique and spectacular by using 'Rub 'n Buff' metallic finishes to create your own personalized design. This also gives a metal finish to wood furniture and will enhance all the wood pieces you paint by adding it to the legs and base of the furniture.

Modern Minimalist Style

Modern Minimalist is the complete opposite of Victorian. This style is a form of extreme accuracy; nothing is too much, without heavy backgrounds. The emphasis is on simplicity, the colors may be dull or bright, in any case flashy colors. Pieces are either geometric shapes – square, rectangular, round, but the surfaces are clean, no scenery, no details. Minimalist modern style by its name, illustrates the simplified forms.

Furniture with clean lines and no extra adornment showcase this style. Blocks of saturated color mix with boxy upholstery with plain legs or skirt less bases.

Lacquered finishes and a mix of woods, both light (birch and oak) and dark (walnut and mahogany) help to create this smooth, clean sophisticated appearance. Geometric or abstract patterns and Pop Art–inspired accessories complete this look.

Indestructible tables with turned legs, trestles, or substantial pedestal bases define this style. Think warm wood tones with rustic or distressed finishes and natural fabrics, like cotton and wool; these fabrics work beautifully with Cozy Casual design styles.

Solid textiles, simple stripes, or unfussy floral patterns in muted colors complete this look.

This style is easily created in contemporary architectural designed homes. Simple, straight walls, many free standing (does not reach the ceiling) angled ceilings and even plant shelving works perfectly for this style.

Windows in the contemporary home are typically long and narrow and lend themselves to no curtains. If yours do not, pick up a couple of rolls of tinted window film. This is an inexpensive idea to provide complete privacy, reduce harmful rays from harsh sunlight and create the minimalist look.

Once applied you will have the same effect you see in commercial buildings. You cannot see in from outside; rather it appears as a mirrored image.

Tiled floors are perfect for the minimalist look. If you do not have a solid surface floor I urge you to take a look at the Victorian chapter addressing tearing up the flooring and painting the subflooring. A neutral blue gray with a poly finish is the look you want to achieve.

Your walls should be painted in light blue grays or shades of muted whites. The woodwork should not create a break visually so try using the same color as the walls in a higher gloss.

Rugs are not necessary nor do they lend themselves to this style. Think minimal!

The furniture is sleek and also minimal. You can repaint or refinish all of your pieces; try using nickel plated spray paint, chrome or high gloss black or white to achieve this look. If your current furniture has decorative trim, remove it before painting. The look will be totally transformed.

Chrome paint is excellent for the legs; switch to a high gloss black or white for the tops of the tables and add sleek hardware to the pieces.

For this makeover begin by painting the walls in washable flat paint. Pale blue grays blend well with the nickel and chrome colors that compliment this style. It is necessary to minimize the ornate woodwork so that it visually fades into the walls. Match the color and use satin or eggshell paint (low sheen) on the woodwork. The ceiling should be bright white and reflect the light down. Standard ceiling white will accomplish this.

If your budget and circumstances permit sanding and refinishing the floors to a neutral light color will work wonders to diminish the visual changes you experience in this room Modern Asian bamboo influenced stain is perfect.

This is light and airy and will blend into the walls. You have an equal stark effect by using a very dark wood stain like espresso. It appears clean and sleek.

Otherwise, white paint will do the job for very little expense

Hanging natural rice paper shades in a color that matches the woodwork will promote a sleeker appearance. Pull them down to the floor to create the long narrow look you want for the windows in the room. These shades are very inexpensive and will accomplish the goal. The shades come in a variety of designs. The simpler look is best for this style.

Look for a piece of furniture that takes advantage of the angles in this room. A half circle piece will totally remove the visual impact of the wall; drawing the eye to the furniture rather than the architecture. The console table pictured is a perfect fit to draw attention away from the bay windows and into the style.

Acrylic is also available for less money; however, a clear acrylic will defeat the intention of drawing attention away from the architecture..

Shopping thrift and garage sales may not be as fruitful for this style as online purchases and Craig's List.

You can use older modern pieces that are readily available at thrift stores and simply paint them to match your color scheme.

Avoid rugs but add texture with clean lines on the sofa accent pillows and accessories. A room without texture is cold and uninviting.

Rustic Style

Rustic is an interesting style. It conjures up thoughts of mountains and sweeping views and crackling fireplaces.

The style structure is crude, featuring rough, natural details; structure elements of furniture and lighting can be in tree trunks, logs, branches, jute. This style is typically found in mountain vacation homes, and rural areas.

If you love the rustic style and live in a log cabin, you're in luck! This is a made in heaven marriage. The images previewed here reflect the typical design of the rooms.

Open spaces, inviting furniture that begs you to curl up and enjoy the view and the fire work perfect in living areas. Even if your furniture is not made out of rough hewn logs, you can substitute this with older heavy solid wood pieces that are found in nearly every thrift store.

Wall colors should be deep and rich; Pine Yellow, Deep Rich Brown and Hunter Green are complimentary to this design style.

Sherwin Williams offers this guide as their Rustic Refined Collection. It is a good place to begin. You can pick up samples of the paint at Lowe's for $3.00 and take them home to try in your surroundings. Avoid very dark colors in small spaces!

Let's take a look at a typical home that is not rustic in design and presents more challenges. Wallpaper may be a quick fix for the walls; it is available now in wood tones, stones and a host of other options.

Limestone brick wallpaper and stone paper is available. You need only decide on your color scheme and then select the pattern that works with it. You can also purchase faux stone and add it to the fireplace area or any area you want to emphasize in this design. Budget permitting you can purchase a rustic mantel or make one. Otherwise, the one shown is a faux mantel and is priced very reasonably.

If you opting for paint, a darker room will benefit from using lighter shades in washable flat paint. Creamy whites or light taupe would work nicely here.

The ceilings should continue the typical ceiling white unless you have really high ceilings; if so, you can paint them in very light beige.

So, let's imagine the fireplace with the faux stone or wallpaper and the walls in a pattern you have chosen. We have almost created our canvas! But, look at those floors!

If you are renting and stuck with the carpet it is time to clean it and cover it up! Rustic rugs like these are helpful. Finding fake bear skin rugs is perfect! You can make these out of fake fur fabric on a foam backing.

These rugs are readily available so just keep your eyes open in thrift stores, online, on Craig's List, almost everywhere!

If it is possible to change the flooring to wood, that is wonderful. If not, you can pick up half inch plywood and cut the planks in. Then secure it to the sub flooring and stain in a natural wood color.

The sliding glass door is clearly not typical to this style. Wooden shutter doors are available for sliders that actually slide! If you match these to the window shutters you will create a truly rustic ambiance. Then add the rugs.

If that isn't possible, opt for tie-up blinds or the rustic look curtains; draping fabric secured with metal rings will accomplish this look.

If you are even a little handy, you can easily locate actual feed bags from your local tractor supply or online and *make them*!

Look for simple pieces of furniture in your house to repurpose. You can paint the pieces in a natural wood color and reinvent them.

Your accessories can be changed by merely painting frames with the bronze and copper spray paint.

Don't be afraid to try this on lamp shades and lamps as well. It works! If your furniture is not rustic and not new, create this by using the hammer and chain technique to 'rough up the surface.' This is accomplished by actually beating the wood!

Apply Minwax in the desired color and you will have rustic furniture. Add baskets and natural accessories to soften the tones in the room.

Classic Reinterpreted Style

This is a refined style, elegant, where classic forms details are found in a new approach. The forms preserves the structure of old forms or parts in general updating them sometimes or some elements of a furniture style combined with modern elements, creating that fusion between old and new. Finishing parts are in a new approach-painted and varnished, with different and innovative colors, surface gold, silver, finished with patina or serigraphic.

This style is actually a new name for Art Deco. You may recognize it better when referred to in that manner. Art Deco was one of the shortest-lived design periods in history.

It is all about sensational, freewheeling modern living and daring new designs. Deco was hit hard by the looming Second World War. It was time to pack up the Charleston records, put away glamorous accoutrements and face harsh reality.

But the style never seems to go quietly, or for long. The reason Art Deco furniture is popular again now is easy to figure. "Art Deco embellishes simple forms, exquisite materials and luxurious finishes to create a truly modern expression. We're comfortable with the familiar shapes and proportions of Art Deco. That's why Art Deco resonates and endures. Art Deco complements both modern minimalism and classic traditionalism.

When we think of Classis Reinterpreted home furnishings, we envision voluptuous leather or velvet upholstered club chairs, sleek lacquered cabinetry, gleaming martini sets and mirrored boudoir vanities. Hallmarks include geometric or rounded silhouettes, inlays and veneers, ornamentation such as starbursts and zigzags, and machine age materials such as aluminum, plastic and steel.

If you're a little bit Artsy, traditional and still love elegance this design style will be a perfect fit for you!

This style can be easily created in almost any architectural setting except typically Rustic designs.

Traditional or contemporary, it is more about the furnishings and the overall finished appearance.

Mediterranean furniture featured very dark wood with ornate trim added for detail. Frequently the sofas and chairs were covered in velvet or 'crushed' velvet.

French Provincial furnishings were typically white or lighter wood tones, many times with gold stenciled trim.

However, they are durable and really beautiful in their repurposed glory. They are much prettier today than in their original state. The lighting is spectacular, if a little bit funky.

You must decide what pieces of furniture you have to work with and what style you want to repurpose them into; then you can create a design plan with color, flooring and wall choices that go with your furniture plans.

Bear in mind that small spaces are better suited to light walls. But, they can be spectacular walls! By glazing over a standard pearl white paint you have created elegance and interest. You can add pre-finished trim pieces to create detail on the walls if that compliments your plan.

This is your chance to mix some of everything you like and call it a plan. If you do not have furniture pieces that will create the look you envision, decide which pieces you can sell and use the funds to replace the pieces. The pieces you are seeking are vintage; their condition is not important since you are going to be refinishing them to a new look.

Shop thrifty for these pieces; it is not necessary to spend a lot of money. You are looking for solid wood pieces with great lines and detail.

The flooring in your home is not going to be an issue as any type of flooring can work with your plan. If you have wood floors and own the home you may want to consider refinishing them to a darker color or to a silvery white. If not, just select rugs that go with the style you plan to create.

Accessories should contrast or blend in this style. This means painting picture frames or staining them into the opposite side of the color wheel. This is a fun, easy and comfortable selection to work in. Enjoy!

Maverick Style

The Maverick style is a part of the modern style and can even join the high tech style we have discussed.

This approach is very inventive, unusual and unconventional. It is young, explosive, and inventive and does not respect the rules. Structure can be obtained by joining pieces, overlapping volumes and volumes twisting colors can be randomly chosen even for the same room, seemingly nothing happens, only part of the eccentricity of this style.

Eccentric is the operative word here. This style may remind you of your old days at college! The Maverick Style begs for unusual and creative furniture and accessories. You may find that you will blend other styles into this design. For instance, you may love traditional but hate the restraints of that style. Or, love contemporary but don't want the fuss and certainly don't want to look like the rest of the people in your crowd.

In that instance you could easily create your own TV media stand with crates or bricks and a board, paint the bricks into a contemporary color and be at the height of this style.

Notice the enclosed part of the shelving units in the picture above. NOTHING is centered or balanced. This personality begs to be different, ingenious and creative. You can literally make something from nothing and decide which additional style you want to blend in with this one.

You may also be intrigued by cutting edge designs that are simplistic and stark but totally different like the chair pictured here.

When looking for items to add to your collection visit furniture stores that carry commercial (office) furniture. You will find this style is plentiful there. These pieces are on the market for resale frequently and do not command a big price. Look past the manner in which it was intended to be used. You will want to think out of the box with this style. Sleek, clean lines with an unusual twist like an unexpected curve will be very pleasing to you. As you look at your own pieces of furniture and accessories try to visualize the same pieces in a beautiful lemon yellow, lime green or sleek black or white.

Chrome is great but if you don't have it currently, a can of spray paint will make that wish a reality! Even if you are working with a wood surface, go for it.

The Maverick Style discards rules. A loft in Soho is equal to a basement apartment. Cutting edge and unusual is what you are trying to create.

Very simple window coverings or a film covering is your best choice. Even in an older home, consider painting the woodwork in a nice silver tone that makes it appear metal and contemporary.

Expose the windows and make them stand out; you are about being different. Blend the woodwork into the wall color. The typical Maverick Style is created from white on white on white for the ceiling, walls and woodwork. But, anything goes!

For this style you would be very comfortable with tiled floors; or equally so with old wood floors. They simply have to be sleek and unusual and cutting edge to get your attention. If necessary, paint the flooring or remove carpet and paint the floor. High gloss is your goal.

For accessories, check out the 70's era and repurpose the pieces with your new color scheme.

It is not necessary to address how to change an unrealistic room into this style, every design works. This style is about clean concise lines and quirky accessories.

Contemporary Style

The room pictured above is actually a modern contemporary style combo but maintains a contemporary line through selected finishes and the color palette used.

The choices of furnishings are very new, modern, and cool. Colors are balanced, warm, bright tones; pastel can be out of the question when it comes to these styles.

The wood finishes are warm, wood-veneer; solid wood doors with frames that appear to look more polished, and panels upholstered with leather or textile materials may be characteristic of this style. Ideal materials are velvet, plush, upholstered pieces. Jungle print or other animal skins are often used in shaping the ambience characteristic of this style.

Steer away from country styles that exhibit printed plates, vegetable or floral colors and stains. They will fall flat in this design. Opt for solid colors with no fringe or designs on the cushions and throw pillows. This style will not be kind to ofa covers or anything that breaks the eye from a long, sleek line.

Seek out Scandinavian modern style furniture and accessories.

Canister or recessed lighting is perfect. In lieu of that, opt for sleek, lightweight pendant lighting, chrome floor lamps that bend and arch and lamps that are simple and sleek in design.

White sofas, white rugs and white accessories blend with the deep rich wall colors or accent walls you may want to create in this style. Chrome and bronze is great, gold is out.

The next picture is a newly constructed home that reflects the contemporary architecture this style is created for. These are very high, vaulted ceilings, tall and wide sweeping windows, recessed lighting and sleek modern furnishings. It is the perfect example of this style.

If you don't have this, build a platform around your bed frame and paint to match your woodwork.

Look for prefabricated nightstands that attach to the wall with no base on the floor. They are inexpensive and really promote this design style. Paint them to match your new platform.

Artwork is specific in this style. Notice the lines and color in this next photo. They are slightly abstract but more free style and modern.

This reflects the style and the colors that blend well with the vibrant accent colors on your walls and throw pillows.

Today's contemporary designs are incorporating darker wood floors with white rugs to complete your new look.

High-tech Style

High-tech style is an innovative modern style, the emphasis being on furniture structure where every detail of combination is not random and it is part of that structure.

Screws, rivets, wheels apparent booms, rough metal finishes, appearances bulbs are specific to this style. The finishes used are often of metal, glass and plastic and wood in small proportions and for parts we find fabric-upholstered as simple as we can, leather. The colors are often dull-gray (brushed nickel), white and small black scale.

High tech is the zenith in contemporary design. It is unusual to simply happen into a home where this is the architectural design unless you have a high rise in a large city. Let's assume you don't and that you need to create it from an average home.

However do we arrive at lighting that will mimic this style? Overhead lighting can be transformed by attaching a strip of sheet metal sprayed with your chrome spray paint. Even a stovepipe will work. This is an extreme canister design. High-tech allows for some leeway in the rough metal finishes.

If you have carpet, tear it out and prepare the floor for painting. You are seeking a high gloss smooth finish. Two coats of poly on the floor will bring a very high gloss finish to the floor.

Bar stools and seating can be made from auto wheels stacked up. Even in the bedroom, you can create a chair form them and add an oversized pillow on top.

The furniture should be painted to a high gloss white, black or red, a little like the Asian without any fuss. Eliminating hardware on the drawers if possible is best. You can use wood filler in the existing holes before painting. If you must have hardware look for the most minimal and sleek design possible.

Your flooring and furniture will create the design in this room. However, if the room is not too small you will want to opt for bold paint colors with a contrasting accent wall in this room. If the room is small, select a bright white for the ceiling, walls and trim. Then choose black or red for your furniture color.

Think contemporary and minimal when selecting throw pillows and window treatments. Sleek fabrics like satin with no design are good window treatments if you cannot use the window film. You are stripping out the whimsy and replacing it with cutting edge, sleek and high contrast.

Elegant Country Style

This style is at the opposite end of the spectrum of High-tech! It features rural and elegant furniture styles with influences from the English, French or Scandinavian classics. Rural chic is a better description.

Furniture finishes are nice, bright colors; white, pastel colors and forms in this era were taking over traditional furniture, but it does not feature abundant decorations. Surfaces are painted or sometimes have a slight patina.

Many people confuse this with shabby chic. The big difference is the period of the furnishings. Shabby chic loves the very ornate pieces as much as the boxy furnishings. Loose pillows and a general country atmosphere typically pervade that style.

Not so for the Elegant Country. Scandinavian lines are clean and sleek. They do feature curves and some stark, interesting detail. This design begs for tailored chair covers, nothing frilly, and tailored simple throw pillows and curtains. Even drapes may be too much unless you opt for very light weight puddled curtains or very sleek white lightweight drapes. Envision country squire; they never want to be perceived as 'country.'

Is fairly simple to recreate this design; look at your furniture. If you have straight lines on the legs you can probably use the pieces. It is easy to change out the color of the furniture by painting or using Min Wax to stain the pieces. If you have wooden floors you are going to want to steer clear of the high gloss maple and oak tones. You want a white bone finish or even a mahogany or espresso finish with white rugs.

Think about adding a piece of inexpensive faux marble to the tops of your furniture in a white or light color with a dark finish on the rest of each piece.

Crystal lamps or accents are very workable in this design. Elegant rather than shabby is your goal in the finished product. If you have the old cherry frames on your pictures, lightly sand the frames and stain them to mahogany or paint them white. Either dark and rich or white and lustrous is a better choice.

You can use some brass or gold accents lightly in your room. Use Rub 'n Buff on your mirror frames and picture frames for a polished elegant and beautiful finish. It comes in a large variety of colors that you may love. You literally apply this with your finger and rub it in or off. I consider this a staple in redecorating. You can use it on lighting also. It works equally well on wood or metal.

Lighting should be soft and elegant; crystal or a combination of milk glass and crystal will dazzle in this style.

Old candlesticks transformed with 'Rub 'n Buff' will be a perfect final touch.

We are looking for soft, elegant and comfortable! Try painting all of the window trim white. Add thick white rugs to the floor and soft sheer white drapes across every window in a clean motion with as few breaks as possible.

The walls should be a pearly white, which is a softer white than this contemporary style typically features. You will need to make covers out of a soft frosted Plexiglas for the inevitable recessed lighting this space features. Then look for crystal chandeliers and wall sconces to soften the stark feeling of the room. Think quality with a soft, quiet elegance throughout the space.

For accessories, a few great pieces are better than a lot of farm house finds. Silver and pewter are excellent accents to this design.

Look at electric fireplaces in a nice white shade at your Lowes or Home Depot and add for ambiance.

Shabby Chic

Soft floral fabrics and accessories, pale colors, and a mix of old and new define Shabby Chic Style decor.

Shabby Chic Style Furniture features time-worn, romantic styling and solid construction, making them just right for those in search of this casual, comfortable style!

Shabby chic is the dumpster divers dream! You can use almost any style except contemporary or modern and convert to this.

Much like the elegant country style, shabby chic is inspired by the English and French classics. This is a beautiful, cozy, comfortable style but also permits a little more fuss in the finished product. I am going to use several pictures just to illustrate the many ways to create shabby chic. This design almost requires you to paint the furniture. You will need to mix white paint with two thirds glaze and apply several coats. No poly for this style. Instead, you will need a hand sander to bring in the distressed look!

Search for old solid wood 6 panel doors and other stay wood pieces including barn siding. These pieces are perfect for creating walls that appear to be wood paneled and yet are finished in the distressed look.

Shabby Chic loves crystal! In the lighting and everywhere, it is a romantic, soft look that loves to pretend to be elegant.

This bath is a perfect example of a modern home gone shabby! Bead board mixes with crown molding to shout, "I used to really expensive!"

This is a perfect example of typical shabby chic room. Notice the simple tables that once were described as early American, now in a new kind of heyday as a beautiful shabby chic accessory!

The old armchairs now have brand new white slipcovers with tie downs exposed. Soft floral designs in pink and pastel purples are beautiful accents. It's really all about white and distressed.

You can use marble tops or simple painted wood pieces just be sure to distress the wood! I highly recommend you seek out crystal chandeliers and lamps. You will love the effect of an electric fireplace if you don't currently have one. It is a soft, simple romantic touch.

If you find one that does not have a mantel, add one even if it is an old used one (better!) or a prefabricated one.

Soft light weight window treatments are a perfect match for this style. You can use the old Priscilla ruffled curtains in a sheer white or opt for the very simple sheer white drapes, I have used white sheets many, many times with great results!

Shabby wants to be elegant. Add tie backs in ornate gold for a beautiful effect. You're going to love this!

Shabby Seaside

Shabby seaside stays with the distressed look of shabby but the lines are much sleeker. Look for more tailored but decorative throw pillows, lighting that incorporates metals, yet remains delicate and nautical teak wood pieces for accent.

For wall colors think of the colors found by the sea; the sand, the craggy cliffs, the seashells, the skies and the sea.

Metal is used in abundance in the table bases and accessories.

Curtains are typically straight sheer panels hung by metal rings. Curtain rods may be metal and exposed.

Follow most of the shabby chic ideas and incorporate heavier weight fabrics, including canvas.

Accessories like frames and lighting can be altered with the same Rub 'n Buff methods described in the shabby chic; the seaside is a darker finish reminiscent of the lighthouse colors.

Southwestern

Southwestern interior design is characterized as rich texture with earth-tone colors as the main palette; using bright accents of yellow, orange, red clay, and turquoise, hand-crafted objects, and terra cotta or clay tile roofs.

Upholstery is predominantly made of woven fabrics, leather and suede's as well as animal hides. Traditional native clothing and blankets may be used as wall décor.

Wood furniture is popular and may also feature a distressed finish with metal accents. Accents can be anything from hand-painted tiles to painted ceramic pieces with roots in 16th century Mexico.

Native American tribal designs and building elements baskets, pottery, rugs and built in niches for artwork are also a common design theme in this architectural style. Southwestern style is very "earthy" and organic, and does not translate well to other indigenous areas of the United States.

Almost every architectural design lends itself to the southwestern style.

If you have selected Southwestern as your choice you will surely want to begin with the walls. You can create a leathered look if you want to faux paint but you can also find the same look in inexpensive wallpaper. Earth tones and more earth tones is the name of this game.

If your room is small, lighten up! Use soft creams and pale gold's on the walls and accent with beautiful turquoise lamp shades.

Exposed natural wood is very desirable to this design style. Rough hewn accent pieces blend naturally with polished hand carved figurines.

Adding faux beams to your ceiling (made from foam and inexpensive) will quickly convert your space.

Vibrant colored accessories that conjure up dessert warmth and Native American heritage set a perfect stage for the southwestern design.

Add natural and vibrantly colored pots and woven baskets to create a warm inviting atmosphere.

Wooden floors are perfect and yet, travertine marble tiles work just as well! For floor coverings I like to steer clear of the 'cow print' rungs and opt for really think wool rugs and vibrant multi colored design rugs.

Accessories and lighting that mimic the silver mined in the west are beautiful in this style.

Window treatments are varied. You can use a simple tie up shade or add natural shutter doors to cover your sliders and then match on the windows.

You have some leeway in the throw pillows as well. You can use vibrant emeralds, ruby reds, soft creams with braid in place of tassels and Native American designs.

Take a look at this old and very traditional piece of furniture that was refinished in a crackle finish. This is a good example of how you can reinterpret existing pieces to this style. The top was covered in faux leather fabric.

If you do not currently have a southwestern motif in your furnishings this is a good example of what you can accomplish.

As you look at your furniture remember you can also distress the existing wood tones for this style.

Southwestern is very comfortable with metal accessories and furnishings. You will see metal often used in the legs and even entire tables made from metal with natural colorful tiles for the tops.

You can pick up several different tiles and break them up and create a mosaic table top for under ten dollars. Use your imagination and enjoy your southwestern style.

Mid Century Colonial

Colonial decorating was rustic, basic and simple. But the period this decorating style covers lasted for around 300 years – so as time went on, and for richer people, the style became more ornate and lavish.

Ten years ago this was the only Colonial style we talked about. How times change! Today we have Island Colonial (previously known as Caribbean) and *Beach* Colonial! You need a pair of track shoes to keep up these days.

Mid Century Colonial design typically consists of dark wood, simple lines (like Hitchcock chairs) wood and metal headboards and heavy, solid wood tables, dressers and chests.

Fireplaces sported heavy hand carved and very substantial design as shown in the picture above.

Crown molding is a must when you are redecorating into this era. If you do not already have wide baseboards you may want to pick up some prefinished carved pieces and add on to your own existing boards. If wood wainscoting is possible in your budget, add it. If not you can use a wallpaper that mimics the wood look and add a trim board. This should stop at 29" up from the floor.

Wood flooring stays the most true to this design. If you don't have it and you can remove the existing flooring you can easily paint the floor and be right into this design.

Many people have ignored the wood theme and used carpeting, simply adding the rugs that depict this era. Many times a simple room size braided rug will work on a bare painted floor, carpet and actual wood equally well.

Walls can be painted in deep burgundies, ruby reds, hunter greens or the tones of butter cream and white. Avoid the modern interpretations of the colors that appear iridescent or patterned on the wall. A low gloss eggshell, satin or washable flat will work best if you use high gloss enamel on the woodwork.

Shop thrift stores, auctions and Craig's List to pick extra pieces up at great prices.

If you intend to paint the furniture you want to avoid any distressed look and any high gloss paints. This is not a 'shiny' era. Natural dark stains are most desirable. Adding white painted furniture will work well as accents.

Look for high back wing chairs and curved back overstuffed sofas to compliment this design.

This picture is a modern interpretation of the old original colonial style. Small prints on the fabric are typical to this era. Wallpaper is frequently used in Colonial styles; notice how this room, which is in a very contemporary home with 18 foot ceilings, has been transformed by adding the crown molding and a soffit with traditional wallpaper above.

Ornate chandeliers were very popular in this era. Mirrors were created in gilded gold frames or natural wood stained into the dark tones of the era.

Island Colonial

For years we referred to this as the "Hemmingway" style. That morphed into the 'Tommy Bahama Style and Caribbean Style." Today it has become "Island Style.

At the height of her reign (from 1887 to 1901), Queen Victoria ruled over the British Empire which spanned several continents. Because of the infusion of Middle Eastern and Asian cultural influences, Victorian style was extremely eclectic, displaying the elegance, opulence, drama and romance of these other more exotic cultures. By the same token, those British subjects stationed in the British Colonial outposts of the Empire that included Singapore, East Africa, India and the British West Indies, brought with them their language, principles of government, architecture and furniture.

But because they were so far from their beloved Isle, when new furniture was needed, the styles and designs that reminded them of home were adapted to reflect life in the tropics. Furniture in the British colonies of Asia and Africa sported traditional tribal motifs and animal prints like leopard and zebra.

In the British colonies of the West Indies, beds, sideboards, tables and chairs often incorporated local materials including rattan and leather. Motifs, particularly floral ones, and even some of the furniture pieces themselves, took on fanciful aspects and elements. The British Colonial Style that emerged from the habit of British Colonials adapting the comforts of home to their new surroundings is richly traditional, with touches of whimsy and the exotic.

Traditional arrow feet and finials are paired with simulated bamboo posts and cane panels, perfectly illustrating classic British Colonial design.

This design is another that can be created in any architectural design. It works best with darker woodwork and wooden floors. If you don't have that, white will set the same tone in the room.

This style works well with overhead fans that mimic woven fan blades or dark blades with bronze trim. If you have a white overhead fan, use bronze or Spanish bronze Rub 'n Buff for all of the metal parts and paint the blades with a wood tone spray paint like mahogany.

Older pieces blend very nicely in this environment. Look for older tables with metal covers at the base of the legs. You can add odd pieces and blend them by using textured upholstered pieces.

We frequently see the palm tree motif, particularly on the Tommy Bahama brands. You may tire of that after a short time. I suggest you opt for nubby textures in soft island colors for your furnishings.

The walls should reflect the typical whitewash look with a softer cream shade more like the sand. You can add some of your original colonial pieces into this style this evolved from the later mid century colonial style.

Bamboo influenced trim on the sofas and chairs have replaced the fussier look of the original colonial. Things lighten up on the islands!

You are creating a more natural setting with this style; it is relaxed and yet elegant. You can add a mosquito net (about $20.00) above your bed to mimic the 4 poster look. These were necessary on the islands.

Woven shades and shutters are perfect for window treatments. Shutter doors are the best option for sliding doors if you have those to deal with.

Accents in teak wood, distressed bronze mirror frames and dark stain or paint on your picture frames will help you arrive at this style.

You can add animal print chairs or recover the seats and make matching pillows from the same animal print. These animals are native to the British Isles.

Any pieces you can find to add that are constructed in natural wood, bamboo and slate are a wonderful addition.

Use candles freely as they finish this style in a laid back, casual and elegant manner.

Brass and bronze can be mixed with a few crystal accents just to give added punch.

Metal is also freely used in the Island Colonial design in lighting and furniture.

Think white wool room size rugs compliment this style, but so do natural woven rugs will very little nap.

Think cozy, elegant, romantic and casual at the same time and you will have created the Island Colonial.

Beach Colonial

The very subtle difference between the Island Colonial and the Beach Colonial are reflected in the billowing curtains, bright white of the walls and accessories and a deviation from the heavier furniture to the almost 'beach like' chaise lounge style chairs. Lighting is now very lightweight pieces in place of the heavy wrought iron; taller, narrower and a little more modern.

In an almost seaside variation, the old crown molding has been exchanged for weathered bead board extending 18" down from the ceiling with a trim board. You can do this if you have high ceilings. If you don't, you may want to try bead board on a single wall.

Chandeliers have actually gravitated to crystal in the beach design plan. Choose the burnished or antique gold bases with a lot of teardrops. Wall scones mimic this same look and make the room feel romantic and airy. If you find pre owned lighting and love it, don't forget the Rub 'n Buff technique to make it yours exclusively! The tiniest bit of this product goes further than you can imagine!

This next photo depicts a dining room using the newer colonial lines with a washed out look to the chairs, better known as slightly 'distressed.'

Beach Island style consists of dark woods, light woods and natural woods blended together in harmony, much like 'beach finds'. Create an overall light and airy feel with bright white walls, light weight fabrics and smooth, clean lines.

Old candlestick sconces blend with new accessories. This style is much freer in the flow of the design. Use your existing pieces and paint some if you like, but refrain from matching the chairs to the tables or anything else.

If using baskets in this design plan pick lighter colors, reflecting a sun bleached feeling.

Where can this be created comfortably? Everywhere; it lends itself to nearly any architectural design style. This design style is about a light filled room, lightweight fabrics that promote that feeling, a collection of simple furniture pieces tastefully joined together to create a casual and inviting atmosphere.

Chapter 9
Sizing It Up

Before ddressing the conversion of your furniture to fit your new dream plan, it seems fitting that we should also talk about the size of your room and what choices will work best to help you create your plan.

Tips for Tiny Places:

Small spaces offer a range of challenges and come in a variety of shapes.

From the graduate exchanging home for a dorm room (and usually sharing it) to studio and efficiency apartment dwellers, cottage or bungalow inhabitants, growing families who are searching for a method to accommodate the changing needs of their family, anyone attempting to find a space for their home office and anyone who lives in a city where space is at a premium with a price tag to match; all of you share this challenge.

A castle does not have to have palatial space to feel like a palace.

Dorm Rooms present a special set of issues. You have one room the size of a typical bedroom that must become the 'home space' for two people, include a place to quietly study, relax, enjoy some privacy and provide enough storage for all the 'stuff' young people deem as vital to their happiness. (This includes clothes, shoes, computers, TV's and everything that applies.)

While many dorm rooms come equipped with some basic furniture they rarely work towards creating a home away from home as they imply.

If you are lucky enough to have a good relationship with your room mate, things can get a lot better very affordably.

Shop thrift stores, Craig's List (Under the 'For Sale' section of Craig's List you will find a Free section. This has postings for 'curb alerts' and will allow you to relieve someone of their goods for the price of your gas to pick it up, and that's all) and any other options you can locate. This is a temporary living arrangement; keep your cash for the lean times and get creative!

Be on the lookout for space saving twin pedestal beds. They take up the same space as the cot you are provided with and offer 6 wide drawers below the bed for expanded storage.

Even if the beds have to be pushed against the wall, you can use the unavailable side for seasonal storage and the important 'stuff' you acquire.

Look for inexpensive open, short shelving units and place them on the closet floor. These will keep spare books, sweaters and jeans easily accessible and leaves the top rod for hanging clothes. Install inexpensive hanging shoe organizers on the interior of the doors.

Search for used night stands that have three drawers. This is not the time or space for the open look. If you do this you will eliminate the need for dressers and open space for one important piece. A desk armoire provides much needed desk space, built in lighting to study, a place for all of your computer and class book storage and, the all important and must have TV. You can close the door and your room is neat; your area privacy is protected when you've finished your work.

Check out the rules on painting your room. If it is permissible, do it! Take a long look at your windows. Adding soft long drapes adds privacy, texture and creates a cozy feeling. They also keep out unwanted natural light when you plan to sleep in! Find complimentary bedding and throw pillows and thick cushy rugs to complete your theme.

Add neutral lamps to the nightstands or opt for wall sconces by the beds to allow each of you the opportunity to sleep without unwanted lights interfering and your tiny, cramped dorm room will become a true haven away from home.

If you have a roommate who is agreeable you will have fun locating these pieces and redecorating. Even the reluctant roommate may have a different attitude when they see your results!

Studio Apartments

These compact units typically consist of one room that accommodates the living and sleeping areas and if you are lucky, a full or partial wall separating the kitchen; and one bath.

Take a moment to review the Dorm Room suggestions to make the most of acquiring storage in your apartment.

You may find a 'Murphy bed' (a fold out bed that appears as a narrow wall unit when closed) is built into the space. If so, it's a great way to get rid of the sleeping area when you're not using it.

If not, you can use the same shopping methods described above to find a used one if you cannot afford a new one.

In lieu of the Murphy bed, a futon is inexpensive, serves as a sofa and folds out to a bed for sleeping. All of these are good space saving options to consider.

Smaller apartment size tables for your living room will allow you to create a spacious feeling in your home. Look for end tables that can double as night stands with three drawers if possible. These will provide storage for clothing and lingerie while serving as end tables during the daytime.

Large, thick wool rugs create a sumptuous and homey feeling in the room and add texture. Look for light, neutral colors to increase the feeling of space. This also adds a visual break point separating your living area from your dining area.

The dining area is probably small, but looking for a way to separate it from your living area will make you feel like it's a special area and not an intrusion into the living space.

Look for a small buffet or entry table to place against the end wall. This adds storage for dining linens and anything else you may need. Again, look for drawers! More is better.

Hang a mirror, a special picture or something simple and large above the buffet. Mirrors make the space feel larger.

Once you determine your personal style, look for a 36" table with chairs that slide under the table. This frees up walking space when you are not dining. If you have space for a small tree beside the buffet you will find that it provides a complete separation of the area visually.

Lastly, go to Habitat for Humanity thrift store, consignment stores or any other option where you can locate a gorgeous light to hang above your table. Nothing says an area is special quite so much as the light you grace that space with.

Top your table with a simple and special centerpiece and your eating area is now a dining area that you will love to entertain in.

The kitchen is usually a galley style that has limited floor space. If a microwave is not included in your apartment look for a small one and hang it under a cabinet. Counter space is critical in galley kitchens.

If you have any available space, look for a rolling cart that doubles as a chopping block/prep area and has storage below. You can move it when you're using it and store it out of the way when you're not preparing or cooking food. Use substantial size baskets on the shelf below to store vegetables and fruits.

The keep it simple method will make you feel much less cramped in smaller kitchens. Orderly cabinets increase storage space; clean countertops allow you to use the limited space for food preparation.

Your bath area is likely to be compact. If so, look around. Is there an area to hang a decorative cabinet and increase storage? If so, find one! The biggest challenge in a studio apartment is find a place for the things you require to be comfortable.

If you have a Burlington Coat Factory or Tuesday Morning store near you, they are worth checking out for shower curtains and inexpensive and attractive storage solutions.

A cloth shower curtain will create a warm and cozy feeling even in a small bath area. Thick towels on the towel bars say 'this is my home.' Some things are worth splurging on and I firmly believe these two items are on the top of the list.

Explore the window coverings and paint options described in the Dorm Room section and apply it to your studio apartment if possible.

Efficiency Apartments

These typically offer a combined living and dining area, a kitchen, separate bedroom and a bath.

Take a moment to review the suggestions in the Dorm Rooms and Studio Apartment sections as they all apply except the sleeping area. You are fortunate to have a completely separate bedroom.

Your bedroom should feel special. You are sharing living and dining spaces; take the time to look for possibilities in your bedroom.

I love to use chandeliers with dimmer switches in bedrooms. You can find really beautiful small chandeliers inexpensively if you shop with the methods we have been discussing in the previous sections.

If that idea does not interest you, look for a really attractive ceiling fan and use the bedside lamps for lighting.

Limit your bed size to a queen unless you have a really large space. Using apartment size furnishings or scaling down the number of pieces in the room will make a dramatic difference in how your room feels.

Paint if possible;find the color and shade that provides the look and feel you want in your private space. Add texture with rugs, window coverings (hang from the top of the wall rather than the top of the window to make the space feel much larger) throw pillows and plants and top it off with bedding that compliments your other selections.

Take a good look at the living room space and the bedroom space and see which best supports a small computer armoire to create your home office.

Your living area will benefit from a TV that hangs on the wall or a narrow media cabinet that increases storage if you do not add the computer armoire.

You may want to explore adding an apartment size sectional sofa. These can create a break from the dining room and living room and still provide an open and spacious feeling while adding seating.

Cottages and Bungalows are actually smaller versions of a typical home. Space planning is more important than ever to achieve a homey, un-cramped feeling.

Eliminate clutter wherever you are able to; clutter is the chief offender of small spaces.

Cottages or Bungalows

Simple, smooth lines will benefit the feeling of spaciousness in your cottage. Sometimes the mere thought of a 'cottage or bungalow' conjures a vision of a Victorian space complete with curly cues on the lamps and curtains replacing cabinet doors. Lose that image!

Cottages benefit from the Seaside and Country Cottage designs that combine soft colors, upholstered furnishings with clean lines and double duty tables in the living room and dining areas.

All of the ideas presented in the 'Dorm Room' sections apply in small spaces. Visit the Efficiency Apartments section to enhance those ides to cover dining and kitchen solutions.

Most of all enjoy the homey and comfortable atmosphere that is gained from a small space! It makes a large statement if you capture the charm and make it yours.

As you are creating your new space, keep these tips in mind. Cramped spaces become creative places and stuffed rooms become stupendous!

Smaller spaces require less of evrything to make a grand statement. Your final goal in the smaller space is to create a feeling of open, airy and inviting. This means lighter colors, bright white ceilings, no dark accent walls, light floring; nothing should break the visual impact except our furniture and the accessories.

Hide woodwork from windows and doorways by using the same color of the light walls in a higher gloss paint. Keep in mind that flat paint hides defects in the walls. High sheen reflects every ding.

If you have a finish on your walls that does not work with your plan, for instance, your plan is for high tech room and your walls are finished in a texture design, opt for the flat paint. You want to literally create a clean canvas and then paint your picture with the furnishings and accessories.

If you have the opposite challenge, you live in a home with a wide open floor plan and your plan requires a cozier atmosphere the following tips will help you arrive at the desired look and feel.

Escaping Open Spaces:

In the last twenty years a 'new' concept of homes became popular. Gone were the square parlors, traditional living rooms, separate dining rooms, isolated kitchens, enclosed family rooms and square bedrooms with small closets! It's all about open spaces now as that trend has continued. The good news for those who like a lille more cozy atmosphere is that this decade the builders have realized too much is tough to sell.

Open spaces deliver challenges and opportunities simultaneously. Here you are, moved into this new and better home that is open from the front door to the kitchen! What to do?

On the up side, you can choose your dining area. Get creative and see what area feels like a relaxing space; one that has the best view and some access to the delivery of the food will create an easy flow and feel natural.

This floor plan typically defines the builder's idea of the dining area by the placement of the chandelier. That's not a game changer for the 'How To Turn Mundae Into Magnificent' warrior.

Lighting is easily changed from room to room if you love the one you're with and with a replacement if you don't.

A note of caution; before you rush out to buy lighting, decide what style, yes style, is your style.

Take a long look at your furniture, your paint selections, your accessories and the look and feel you want to create in each room.

Lighting is one of the most strategic tools in the game plan of creating your masterpiece. Use it wisely to define an entry area, a dining area and any other 'specific' areas in this floor plan.

In this kind of floor plan, living rooms usually need to be created by furniture selections and placement.

Open floor plans are devoid of wall outlets except against the walls which, as you may have noticed, are missing. Attempting to use table lamps will leave you with exposed cords that impede traffic flow and create unnecessary fall risks.

These floor plans work better with floor lighting and wall sconces that promotes a more comfortable and cozy atmosphere.

Storage is another challenge in the open floor plan. Decide whether you want to create an entry area or foyer and work from that point of beginning.

Placing an entry chest or buffet style of furniture at the point where you want to 'end' the entry area will provide a place for paper and pens to jot down notes or messages at the door and a place for sweaters and other light wraps you grab on the way in or out of your home.

Open shelving units will maintain the open feeling, create a break point and still provide some light storage if drawer units are located in the bottom sections. We'll be looking at furnishings and where to find the things that best suit your design ideas later in this book.

This same challenge is encountered in the family room area and can be addressed in the same manner. The best part of an open floor plan is the walls you do not have to relocate!

The open floor plan usually offers "plant shelving" to accommodate floating walls. These become a display area for your most valued treasures that are stored in many attics for lack of a place to show them off safely.

And one more thing; if you have vaulted ceilings you now have very tall walls. Make good use of them! Look for shelving or older free standing cabinetry units, repurpose them and 'hang 'em high!'

This is a wonderful place to showcase something important in your décor plan.

You can find every style of pre-built fireplaces at your local Lowe's and many other places (back to the online search here) and create your best focal point by placing it under a hanging unit.

You also acquire that much talked about mantle for hanging stockings and a romantic setting for the cozy evenings with this kind of unit. They also have a heater and blower hidden behind the glowing 'fire, making them a very practical solution to a cold room!'

It's a given that having an unlimited budget leaves every door open in your selection. If not, take heart; we have a plan!

We will be devoting a few chapters to furniture placement and how to create specific and defined areas in your home. Those chapters may be very beneficial to you.

Chapter 10
Walking the Walk

Great changes have been forced on almost every corner of the planet as we experience a pandemic shutdown of life as we have known it. Tens of millions of jobs have been interrupted; homes have become offices, schools, gyms, playgrounds and every function we once left the home to get to. Now, more than ever, it is obvious how important using the space effectively is.

I love this next story and frequently include it in books and discussions, because it applies over and over again in life. At some point we are all forced to make changes and re-evaluate what we once considered normal in our lives. Before we get to the exciting stuff, like finishing the transformation and your furniture, I would like to tell you a story that may be of assistance as you choose your pieces to work with.

'Once upon a time, in a very prosperous kingdom, a district was referred to as 'Barely Get Along Street;' the area was filled with homeless, hapless individuals who had not yet learned to be prosperous.

Others in the Kingdom frequently 'threw them a dime' and donated their cast offs to this area. And, so it was that no one wanted to be associated with 'Barely Get Along Street.'

That was then, this is now! The 'Barely Get Along Street' district has become hip and chic. It *rocks!*

The residents in the kingdom wasted many opportunities and fell into the trap of complacency and soon their prosperity was siphoned off, knights lost their commission in the royal palace and a pall fell across the entire kingdom.

Although everyone was affected, the people who knew best how to navigate this state of affairs all seemed familiar with the 'Barely Get Along Street' District.

As they watched their comings and goings much was written about the people in this area. The perception that they had no choice was quickly replaced by the knowledge that they had made a better choice!

These residents found great value in the 'stuff' other people tossed without a thought.

They looked harshly at waste and pollution of the kingdom and beyond, and worse still, their homes were just as nice as the highest family in the royal hierarchy.

They dressed nicely and had little or no debt for the collector to come knocking at their door demanding their hard earned dollars.

All across the kingdom residents began to watch how these people operated in their daily lives; it was the dawn of a new era!

One where we are all responsible for our actions and where hands that reached out were touched in a beautiful way by people who had never before reached out!

Dumpster divers posted their wares at a place called Craig's List; and their goods were very valuable and affordable!

No longer were there cast offs with a long life time yet to be lived stacked into a disposal pile.

Someone fell in love, again, and the cycle of recycle became the norm.

Thrift stores popped up at every corner of the kingdom, even near the palace. Owners whose efforts were not successful in selling their goods consigned them to a better salesperson.

At every turn in the kingdom the residents were treated with the opportunity to find better quality items at more affordable prices and; to make them theirs! How you may ask?

By repurposing! Everyone's doing it now. We have discarded the idea that new cheap particle board furniture is preferable over used furniture!

The savvy buyer today looks for great quality, sturdy wood and a look and feel they can relate to.

They take it home and change it to fit their own dream home plans and the cycle continues.

Debts were cleared from the books in the kingdom; families began sharing time together repurposing their new finds and laughter once again permeated the kingdom!

This resulted from the diminished stress the residents of the kingdom were feeling, having tossed the notion that they had to 'be' anything accept what they were comfortable being. And life was good again!

The most recognized shopping spots in today's 'Barely Get Along Street' districts are eBay, Goodwill, Salvation Army and Craig's List.

These are quickly joined by Habitat for Humanity Thrift Stores, other thrift stores, consignment stores, yard and garage sales and classifieds in your local newspaper.

Once you see what terrific finds are available you will be inspired to join as a seller to repurpose your pieces that no longer fit.

Ah! There is joy in the kingdom!

A word of caution:

Do not make buying trips to a strangers home or invite strangers to your home for selling items alone. Ask a friend or neighbor to join you. There is safety in numbers! If you feel anything odd about the transaction use your shoes to win the battle and walk away. 'Gut instinct' has saved many a person from a bad experience!

NEVER send payments by Western Union or any other method to a person you cannot meet or to a place you cannot get to or in.

Discard any ad or response that relates a sad sack story about the person having to leave the country but keys etc. will be mailed to you. They won't.

I avoid any Craig's List ad that does not include a telephone number. I rarely respond to emails. Let them call you. You can make a better judgment on who you are dealing with if you hear their voice and the sincerity as they talk with you.

Don't accept checks or money orders for payments. My youngest son has just given his second vehicle away, complete with title to a stranger who first gave a Postal Money Order and the last time produced a Cashier's Check.

Both were worthless paper. Both are hopeless situations for him. These crimes are rarely solved.

If your buyer is not comfortable bringing all the cash, accept a deposit and let them bring it back when they pick up the item.

Don't set yourself up for a failure, or for unnecessary danger.

If your budget is nearing the bottom of the barrel keep a vigilant watch on the For Sale 'Free' section of Craig's List. Many people discard really good pieces by posting a 'Curb Alert".

These people do not have the time or the inclinations to attempt a sale but are happy to see someone who can use their things take them away. Imagine!

Personally I have never a bad experience with curb alerts. The price tag alone (FREE) suggests this is a good deal!

When you visit a consignment store, don't hesitate to make an offer; this is especially true if you are making multiple purchases. Consignment prices should always present a value hoped to attain. Keep this going! Join the sellers queue and collect the value from your items to add to your decorating budget; or donate the items to worthy resellers.

It's a little like early American barn raisings, where neighbors help neighbors and everyone is a pioneer! Skid Row morphed into Skid Rose (as in rose from the ashes!) And all was well again!

And so you see, "Once Upon A Time" has become "Once upon a choice!"

Chapter 11
Supersized Dreams

It's time to don your magician's hat and pick up the wand! If you have decided you simply do not have the furniture pieces that you are comfortable with recreating and don't have funds to purchase the right pieces, decide whether you are willing to sell them to raise the capitol to purchase the right pieces. If so, the last chapter has a wealth of information on how to accomplish that goal.

Refinishing furniture is an old art and not at all intimidating or cutting edge. Detailed instructions on how to achieve the 'finish' you want are available online by a simple search.

This is more about how to take the pieces you have to work with and recreate them into the 'style design' you have chosen. It is a bigger challenge and a lot more fun. In fact, it is downright exciting when you see the results!

Take a good look again at your design style and note what things most appeal to you about that style. This is important in the recreation process. Was it the colors, the smooth or ornate feeling, the overall ambience… this is a personal choice but the 'whys' matter.

Surface finishes are easily accomplished by using liquid sand. Distressed or shabby designs require lightly sanding the wood afterwards, applying two coats of white primer, applying a coat of crackle in medium blend if desired and adding your color choice. A final light coat of antiquing glaze was applied to bring out the crackle and wood grain.

New hardware more suited to your theme should replace the original.

When doing this, fill in the previously drilled hardware holes with wood filler before you begin if you plan on changing hardware.

Looking for a small statement piece? A single primer coat and three coats of deep ruby red paint applied with a brush to a side table, topped off with antique glazing, applied lightly creates an exciting change from typical wood tones. This works well with many design styles. Change the hardware to reflect your new design plan for the room and this little treasure will rise, quite literally, from the ashes to become a beautiful accent piece in the room.

Converting to a Seaside Cottage look? Light sanding and three coats of bright white paint with a clear coat overlay will complete this transformation.

Cozy country style can come to life beautifully by covering the top of an armoire or large piece of furniture in 6 inch lace creating an old, antique design. Then coat with poly. Apply the same lace to the top of each drawer after the initial painting of the piece.

Creating geometric or square requires using painters tape. Create your design free hand, finish in a gold high gloss. This is perfect for the artsy look the owner was trying to achieve.

Old Duncan Phyfe tables have lost a little of their luster on the decorating scene. This is typical and it will make a return, but for now, they are easy to come by and coast very little considering the quality of construction.

Sand or apply liquid sand, wipe off and a 'Min Wax' wood tone or paint color that makes the statement you are creating. You can easily achieve this by using a base coat with a golden base, topping off with a teal color and sanding the corners and legs lightly to arrive at the desired distressed look if desired.

To create a sideboard for your room locate and old dresser or desk, French Provincial is a favorite of many, and paint only the highlighted sections. Then add your final finish to protect the wood.

You can easily find older dressers and desks at almost any place where used furniture is sold for pennies on the dollar of the original cost. You can totally transform an old discarded piece of furniture into the very piece you need. There is almost nothing you cannot do to achieve the look and feel you need in your space from the pieces you have at hand or are able to locate by searching for free pickup, disposal at the road and thrift stores and auctions.

Look closely at the hardware on some of the older pieces. They are beautiful and may become a part of your new design style. Use liquid sand to loosen all the old paint and then sanded with a hand sander.

These are perfect blank canvases to work from. They do not require drawer pulls; this means they can work with modern, contemporary or even high tech if the finish is in high gloss silver or black paint.

You have been reading a lot about the 'Rub 'n Buff' product in this book. Any stain that you are comfortable with is fine. This product is just overly simple to use.

Although it is advertised for metals and is a great fix for that, take a look at the effect on an old cheap wooden chest.

This requires no sanding, no painting, just a simple application process with appliqués applied.

Min Wax is another product that has been highly recommended. I always keep it on hand. Take a look at simple fixes with this product:

You can use to simply bring back the former richness of the original stain.

What about the overall room change? Let's take a look!

Simple! The wallpaper was removed, the mantle was taken off, and the fireplace surround brick was removed and replaced with a very simple wooden handmade trim. The floors were painted in an espresso finish and a contemporary room size run added.

This owner opted to sell the existing pieces of furniture and used the proceeds to pick up inexpensive contemporary pieces.

Before, the room was very traditional and tired. A simple coat of paint on the cabinetry and the addition of a new chandelier in place of the ceiling light fixture produced this result!

Think outside the box!

We can't end this chapter without looking at a bath that has been transformed! Plumbing and electrical was not changed; but look at it now!

This is dark, dingy and totally uninviting. In the makeover, a tub insert with 'prefinished tile look' replaced the shower, the woodwork and vanity was painted and the old commode was replaced. Can you even imagine?

Chapter 12
Balancing Energy

Some people have good ideas about furniture arrangement, almost a "knack' for making things look nice. Others feel lost and helpless. Regardless of which one of thee descriptions fit you; the real golden rule is to smoothly move the energy flow through your home.

This allows people to move comfortably through the space. Even if you feel overwhelmed with the possibilities and insecurities of furniture arrangement the following tips will help you create a successful space.

So, if you are naturally great at this then you probably have a good understanding of how energy moves. On the other hand, if you find yourself standing in the middle of the room, shaking your head and wondering where to begin, this is it!

Although I can't tell you where you should put what furniture, I can provide some insight with questions which will help you think about how you will use your space and some general guidelines for arranging furniture.

How you use your space:

Look at the entrances to the room. Do you have doors? Do they open in or out? If they open in, you will need to allow room for those to open fully.

Do you use the room as a pathway to another room? Is the room a destination room? In other words, is the room one that people go TO or go THROUGH? If they go through, you need an easily navigable pathway from one room to another.

How do you want to feel in the room? Do you want it to be cozy and intimate? Do you want an open and spacious feel? Furniture in a cozy room tends to be places in closer groups. An open feel needs more space between pieces.

Are you going to use the room for entertaining? If so, you need flexibility in your furniture choices. Extra seating may be placed out of the way and be moved into use when company comes.

Furniture Placement Guidelines:

Between the sofa and side chairs, designers normally allow 48 to 100 inches. But you should adjust the space according to your family's needs. If you feel more comfortable with the chairs closer, or if you are better able to hear conversations, then move them closer.

If you are using a coffee table in front of the sofa, the normal placement is 14 to 18 inches from the sofa. But again, if you have short arms or long legs, adjust the table until you are comfortable.

For television watching, the normal guideline is to place the television at three times the size of the screen. But with some of these new big screen TVs, three times the size of the screen is in the next room!

Three feet of space is recommended for traffic lanes. But if you have large family members or lots of kids, I would recommend allow an extra foot for safety for your furniture and for your family members.

In the dining room, an average adult needs a depth of 20 inches for a dining room chair, plus 16 inches to scoot the chair back from the table. Again, adjust the measurements to fit your family.

At the dining table, you should allow 24 inches per person or more. If your family tends to gesture as they eat, as mine does, allow another six inches.

In order to serve your guests, allow 46 inches between the wall and the dining table.

For ideal bed placement, allow at least 24 inches between the bed and the wall to get out of bed comfortably and allow 36 inches between the end of the bed and the bedroom or bathroom door.

As you can see, these guidelines are approximate and should be adjusted for your family. Keep in mind, however, that if you are entertaining guests, your placement will require further adjustments for their comfort and ease of movement.

Small Spaces:

If you can stand in the middle of your room and touch the walls on all four sides, you are going to have to use some magic to add visual space to your room. While that magic probably won't involve the overnight makeover of your space by budget decorating elves, here is some slightly less than elfin visual ideas to help your room look larger:

Light Values: Use light values when painting your room. That does not mean you are doomed to white walls! Try light green or cream beige for a feeling of space.

Vertical Space: Use vertical space for storage. Add a hutch or floor-to-ceiling bookcases as a storage solution to reduce the amount of floor space taken.

Up Against the Walls: Place the larger pieces of furniture against the walls, so the open space in the middle isn't broken up.

Open Arms: Choose a sofa and chairs with open arms and exposed legs. This allows light to filter under the furniture, making the room appear airier.

Scale Down: Consider smaller scale furniture. A sofa or bed that takes up less area will help visually open the room.

Reflections: A large mirror in the room will reflect light around the room. This is especially effective with near a window so the outdoors can be reflected.

Angles: Arrange furniture at an angle if possible. This gives visual interest to the small space.

With some imagination and some rearranging of furniture, you can make any room appear much larger than its actual size.

More Room Design Tips

Furnishing a small dining room can present a challenge, as any small space can be challenging. However, you may very well end up having a more efficient and attractive space since a small dining room can force you to focus on exactly what you need.

Consider Scale

Scale might very well be the single most important factor to consider especially when you are furnishing a small dining room. Your dining furniture should be scaled according to the space you have.

Select a Limited Color Palette

A limited color palette may be a good place to start. It is easier to work with a lighter or neutral color palette as it can make your room look airier. Contrasting or complementary colors should only be used as accents.

This is the safe approach. If you are confident around colors, a bold color scheme may work just as well. The trick is not to get too fussy, and just keep it simple.

Use Mirrors

A mirror is a small room's best friend. It opens up space like nothing else. Use strategically placed mirrors on the wall. Using more than one can be an even better idea.

Decide on Simple Window Treatments

Simple window treatments help keep fussiness away. Ornate swags and valances could be distracting and too overpowering in a small space. Simple panels could do the job nicely. If you need more privacy, layer with good quality blinds.

Select the Best Table Shape

A round table is the best pick for a small dining room. You might want to pick one with an extension leaf if you have enough space to open it. Otherwise a simple round table will do in a square room.

Pedestal bases are great because you can fit extra guests around the dining table without table legs getting in the way.

A narrow rectangular table might work well in a narrow dining room. The idea is to leave enough space for people to move around easily.

Pick Armless Chairs

Armless chairs work best in a small room as arm chairs require more room. You might also want to pick chairs that have a more slender profile. The idea is to take up as little physical or visual space as possible.

Consider Transparent Furniture

Transparent material such as glass, Plexiglas, or acrylic can make your dining furniture "disappear" leaving you with lots more visual space. Remember, though, that this is more about appearances than anything else. You will still need to measure to make sure that you leave enough space for people to maneuver easily.

Use a Small Profile Chandelier

A large or fussy chandelier could take up too much visual room. Pick something with simpler lines and a small profile. It would make your space appear larger. Remember it is all about scale.

Arranging furniture is mostly about using empty space around your furniture to create flow in your floor plan. You want people to move around comfortably without bumping into furniture and sit down comfortably without grazing their knees or feeling hemmed in.

Living Room

For your living room to be comfortable, make sure you don't crowd your space. Too much furniture crammed into too little space or sparse furnishings in a room that is too large can make for a very unattractive space.

You need to provide enough space for an efficient flow of traffic, and let your space breathe visually.

This creates a sense of wellbeing and relaxation.

Traffic Lane: 3' or more
Foot room between sofa or chair and edge of coffee table: 1'6".
Floor space in front of chair or sofa for feet and legs: 1'6" to 2'6".

Dining Room

To enjoy your dining room to the fullest, make sure you leave enough space around the table so that people can get in and out of their chairs comfortably and the person who is serving can move around the table without trouble.

Space for occupied chairs from edge of table to back of chair:
1'6" to 1'10"
Space to get into chairs: 2'6" to 3'
Traffic path around table and occupied chairs for serving: 1'6" to 2'
If you're using armchairs, remember to add two inches to the measurements.

Bedroom

In a bedroom, place furniture so that you don't stub your toes should you need to get up in the middle of the night.

You should also be able to move around comfortably to make the bed and be able to open any drawers without trouble.

Space for making bed: 1'6"
Space between twin beds: 1'6" to 2'6"
Space in front of chest of drawers: 3'
Getting into or out of bed: 2'6"

Around the House

Leave enough space around the doorways, or the room may look very unwelcoming, and crowded. You always want to leave a small transitioning area uncluttered by any furniture when moving from one area of the home to another.

Space from doorway to first object: 3'
Space around main entrance: 4'

Just because you live in a small space it doesn't mean that you have to use small furniture. You will find that many times, using large pieces when decorating small spaces can actually make a room look larger, rather than smaller.

Using a lot of small pieces of furniture can make it look like you're trying to cram too much in and the room can end up look cluttered and cramped. The key to keep this from happening is to use large furniture, but just use less of it.

For example, in a tiny living room rather than trying to fit in a sofa, chairs, ottoman, coffee table and side tables, try using a sofa, a single table or bench, and perhaps a single side chair. If you have the space you can even include a large armoire for storage.

Get rid of excess small pieces and instead include only what you'll actually use. Then try to open up the space with an oversized mirror on one wall (if you can get it across from a window so much the better).

It sounds crazy but it works. Before trying it out; draw up a floor plan on some graph paper or use an online floor planner to experiment with furniture placement.

Simple fixes for small spaces can help you maximize every single inch of your home. The three things that you most need in a small space are function, comfort and style so before you buy anything make sure to look for pieces that provides these three.

Go Vertical: Consider investing in tall furniture. Floor space is precious, and by going upward instead of outward you give yourself extra room.

Use Walls: By adding shelves or wall mounted cabinets you give yourself room for display or storage without using up extra floor space.

Stylish Storage: Buy occasional and coffee tables that provide storage with drawers and shelves. Beds, room dividers and ottomans are some other pieces of furniture that can provide you with extra storage.

Decorative boxes and storage bins can also store seasonal clothing, sporting goods, office supplies or anything else.

Stackable Chairs: Stackable and folding chairs are an excellent way of keeping a supply of seating that you can pull out as you need.

Retractable Doors: Retractable doors that don't open out let you fit armoires and entertainment centers in small spaces with ease.

Try the Kids' Department: Creative use of youth furniture can serve you well as it is designed to fit into smaller rooms. It can also accommodate most adults just as well. For instance, a child's dresser or desk can fit into small areas. And with today's wide selection of styles you are bound to find a piece that matches your own.

Look for Wheels: Many pieces of furniture have wheels, upholstered ones as well as tables and shelves. The ability to easily move your furniture around to where you need it can serve you well.

Consider Leaves: A full-size dining room table might be too big for your dining area. Look around for one that has removable or retractable leaves.

Even though all of these issues were covered in various places in this book, a handy dandy reference guide makes things move swiftly if you're in a bind!

Chapter 13
Wrong Choice Right Place

It's always rewarding to look back when your project is finished. This book was written to help you take a new look at old places or spaces in your home. Our time has been committed to learning how to see things with a different perception and how to turn them into what we needed to create something that feels beautiful again; to you.

It is easy to find something that seems wonderful in the stores and load it up. The dilemma comes when we place it in the exact spot we envisioned it and then suddenly we believe we made a bad choice. There usually are not any bad choices, just wrong places.

One of the most common errors in acquiring furniture is seeing the pieces in a much different space/size than you have to work with. Furniture stores are 25,000 to 50,000 square feet. Things seem very cozy in their settings but may never fit in your own home as shown.

Don't fall for matched pieces; mix wood tones and a little design style change for a more dramatic effect.

It's good to stand back and look critically at your home and notice the way people move through it, watch the looks on their faces in specific areas and you will see that some areas make people smile, some make them relax and some make them feel energized. You can see their footsteps pick up!

We have been working together on how to turn your existing choices into the perfect choices and then making the right best choice in where to place them comfortably in your home. When you have achieved this, you will feel good when you enter the space. It will either give you a warm hug, a burst of sunshine, a gentle smile or something more.

This is the real trick to a beautiful home!

About the Author

'Mining the Mine' is the third book in the 'Make It Mine' series.

Alexa earned a well-respected reputation as a commercial and residential Design Specialist with a career that began in 1976 and continues through today.

Her home creations helped to create winning residential development projects from Ohio to Florida, most notably remembered by her ability to work with each home buyer to create a home that reflected their unique personality showcased in an elegant and natural design.

Alexa's commercial designs included award winning and much celebrated retail store window and floor displays that were photographed and filmed by an international audience while frequently drawing gasps of surprise and awe, always bringing unsurpassed sales.

Her notable skill in conceptual decors has earned her a reputation as a premiere decorator. Her work was noted in Who's Who in American Women in Business and Industry over several years.

Alexa's passion for home decor is reflected in the beautiful surroundings that she creates.

Her ability to collaborate with architects, her own group of contractors, and her clients have earned Alexa a well deserved reputation as a true professional.

Born and raised near Cincinnati Ohio and re-locating to Florida in 1999 she continued her pursuit of decor and real estate development in Fort Myers and throughout south Florida, now residing in Fort Myers Florida.

The release of 'Drowning In My Tears' in April, 2012 was her first venture into the Crime Thriller genre. It was named Book of the Month and on two occasions 'Pick of the Week.'

You may also enjoy 'How to Find YOU in Your Home,' released in December 2012 and 'Sign It' released later the same month.

'Sign It' is a Design by Your Birth Sign book that begins with the nursery and continues through adulthood, including a special chapter about changes that you need to make to ensure the safety of your beloved elderly friends and relatives.

Visit Alexa Keating at www.arkconnect.com.

Alexa Keating

www.ingramcontent.com/pod-product-compliance
Lightning Source LLC
Chambersburg PA
CBHW070651290526

45790CB00001B/271